# Psychology And Investment

# Psychology And Investment

*Author*

**Ajay Srivastava**

ISBN: 978-93-5578-405-6

Published by:

**Ajay Kumar Srivastava**

45, Awas Vikas Colony, Betiya Hata,

Gorakhpur – 273001 (U.P.), India

Mobile No.: +91-9867837184

First Edition, 2022

Price: ₹ 445

Printed by; The Print Company, Mumbai, India

# Lord Jupiter

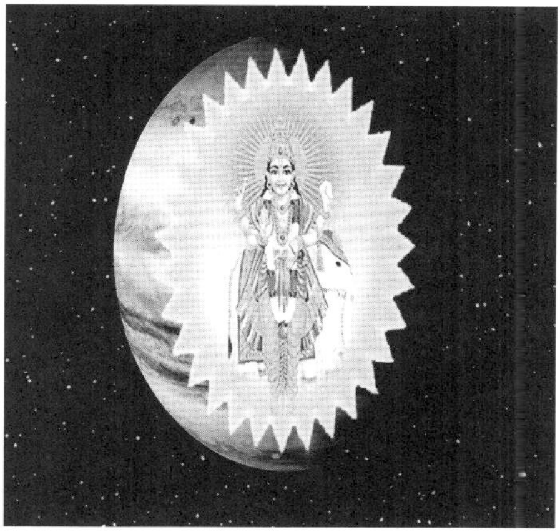

**Prayer**

देवानां च ऋषीणां च गुरुं काञ्चनसंन्निभम्।

बुद्धिभूतं त्रिलोकेशं तं नमामि बृहस्पतिम् ।।

|| Devaanaanca rishinaanca gurum kaancana sannibham

Buddhi bhutam trilokesham tam namaami Brihaaspatim

Om Gurave Namah ||

(**Translation**: I bow down to Jupiter, teacher of gods and sages, the greatest treasure, and the most intelligent of all creation. Om, I bow down to Jupiter.)

# Dedication

I dedicate this book to my father (Late) Sri R.A.L Srivastava who taught me to be an independent, courageous and determined person, and my mother Maya Srivastava whose unconditional love and support always help me to overcome all the obstacles in my life. She has a selfless spirit and served others throughout her life. Her immense patience is peerless and she always inspires me to go ahead.

# Preface

Psychology plays an important role when it comes to make a decision as the matter of investment is a significant matter and it is not just about crunching the numbers. Behavioural economics states that people are not always rational when it comes to make an important decision, and while taking a decision our mind is influenced by various other factors. People are unable to make a proper decision due to; lack of proper information, failure to analyze the situation properly, an unwillingness to learn from their mistakes, constraints of mind or not having enough knowledge about the subject, etc.

Knowledge about the subject alone is not sufficient enough to make a good investment decision. The study of the human mind and behaviour and how it relates to and affects the process of investing is not only important but also very interesting because each person takes the same types of investment differently.

At times the stock market moves irrationally where the numbers do not support the trend. In such situations, psychology helps us to recognize the erratic behaviour of the market and clear the way for any decisive action. Knowledge of the subject can be learned by reading books but overcoming emotions requires both knowledge and experience and the experience of loss is more important than gain.

When I started my career as a research analyst at a business news channel, I had the opportunity to meet various kinds of investors and market experts. Later when I moved on different profiles, I carefully observed that psychology matters most to everyone before making any investment decision. Human sentiments deeply influence the decision-making process and it is very difficult for an investor to take any such action that is not influenced by their surroundings.

Psychology is closely related to investing and when people fail to understand human behaviour, they make wrong investment decisions. The functioning of the mind influences every investment move and the beginning is associated with various characteristics of human emotions such as greed, fear, and many other attractions and resistances.

In this book, I have explained in detail what are those attractions and resistances which I observed while dealing with different types of persons. I felt that the time has come to share my experience with the readers that how psychology impacts us deeply while making investment decisions and with a better understanding of how we can avoid ourselves from taking wrong decisions.

The second part of the book deals with how to analyze a company because apart from investment psychology, knowledge of finance is also important. We hope that this work will be able to throw some light on the complex world of psychology and investment.

I give special thanks to my younger brother Abhay Srivastava and my friend BN Rahul for their valuable suggestions, without which such work would not have been possible.

Ajay Srivastava

06-Aug-2021

# Acknowledgement

The existence of this book would not have been possible without the help of my wife Seema and my daughter Saanvi. They provided me enough help to write down my thoughts which I have collected so far in my life. My wife has been instrumental as an illustrator and proof-reader and has given me enough insights to write the matter in a simple and explanatory manner.

Ajay Srivastava

# CONTENTS

## Part – I: Psychology

## Part -II: Investment

# Part I

# Psychology

## Chapter 1

# Independent Thinking

We live in a society where we are always surrounded by different types of information. Due to technological advancement, now it is a matter of few clicks and the information is in front of us. Now a days this happens in almost every sphere of life, whether looking for any investment product or anything else. After going through the available information, we understand it in our way and make the investment decisions accordingly. During this process, we never think that our decision is influenced by this freely and widely available information.

In India, during the decade of 90s, when investors or traders needed information about the latest price quotes of the stocks, they need to visit the broker's boardroom but now it is available at every home, at every office, on streets, and every city and town.

Media plays a vital role to spread information. After the advent of smartphones and the internet; online data, chart analysis, or any news related to any stock is now in our hands with just a few clicks. Financial news channels provide all the latest information every day, start from the morning with various expert opinions and all the latest developments.

All this freely available information now gives the general public access to reach a large chunk of data that was earlier available to only a handful of people. We never thought that this easily accessible information has a strong capacity to influence our decision-making process. We cannot stay away from the current environment and it is also true that we have to decide on the basis of available information whether we will go ahead with making such investments or not.

For example, let's say you researched a stock over the weekend and decided that on Monday I would invest my money in such a stock. The next day you called your broker and told him about your decision to buy this stock. Before calling them, you were ready that this investment is for your long-term investment. Immediately you get his free advice that whatever option you have chosen will take a long time and he has other stock ideas and you should consider that.

Within seconds he will send various freely available information to you and with proof that whatever path you are going to choose, it will take a lot of time. Invest in these stocks that he is recommending. From his source, he has authentic news that the stock will reach the recommended target price. Soon, you will be sure that 'Yes', he is right.

What he did, he allures your temptation, and you immediately forget about your weekend research and plan. There is a strong possibility that you will put your money as per his advice. You are very happy when within an hour he will call you saying that prices are up from your buying price and do not worry he has news from various authentic sources, the target is just coming.

While researching on the weekend you were thinking about long-term investment, but with this freely available information he can convince you, and now you are interested in short-term gains.

At the end of the day, you feel very happy again with your broker's call that prices have closed higher than your buy price. He will further say that the next day he will be out of stock and will not wait for more.

But what happened on the next day, stock opened in red, you started getting frustrated, your losses are increasing and the whole day you wasted on worthless discussions. There is a strong possibility that you will exit from the stock suffering from losses. The actual process may happen in a day, in a week, or in a month, but the ultimate result is only loss.

I have seen that people hold such stocks for years that they bought only for a day and now waiting to exit at least on their buying price. Unintentionally their short-term investment has become a long-term investment and waiting to exit only at par.

What has happened in this case?

- Why does your long-term investment suddenly become a short-term investment?

- Why do you forget that you worked hard over the weekend?
- How can you be convinced of such short-term temptation?
- Why did you suddenly lose all your thinking?
- What happens to the goals you were planning when you did your research?

We all have human weaknesses and the temptation for making quick money is one of the greatest. Your broker arouse such temptation and you decided to jump in that direction where you have no idea, and on the belief that your navigator for this short-term journey is a highly experienced person.

What did you lose?

- You lose to think independently
- You have lost faith in yourself
- On the belief of others, you decide to take such risk that they will protect you from any negativity

Your broker is getting a commission on every buying and selling of stocks and you are thinking that he is a well-wisher of your money. He is interested in his commissions. But, if the investor has lost his money, then there is an actual loss of the broker too because for further commissions he has to look for another client. A successful broker is one, who never gives any short-term tempting advice to any client. He is interested in the financial well-being of the client and always avoids hot impulses.

This freely available information has great power to mould your thinking process and you may be bound to act accordingly. You cannot acquire the power of independent thinking in a day. It is a gradual accumulation. You can make money only by your efforts, not by the efforts of others. We will discuss further what are the other key factors that influence our minds.

### 1.1 Hot News and Price Quotes

Our mobile phones are flooded with various kinds of news, and when we wake up early in the morning many people's first temptation is to see their mobile. They have a strong desire for news and price quotes. Gradually they get addicted to all these. From morning till late night their discussion point is only hot news and prices of the stocks. Like an addict, they gradually become addicted and at times it is very difficult for such people to keep themselves away from such an environment. They feel very difficult to spend time with family or friends on weekends or during leisure hours.

Sometimes, a long weekend is like a hell for them. Because their nervous system demands their drugs (hot news and price quotes) which are currently unavailable, therefore, they are unable to enjoy the time and feel very lethargic. Their faces shine again when the market opens after a long weekend.

All kinds of addictions are bad, be it in the form of hot news and price quotes or some other. If you are addicted to something then you are taking poison inside. Intoxication is increasing due to your every action and poison is getting accumulated somewhere inside. After some time, the treatment of this poison becomes necessary.

People do intoxication to run away from the situation. The market knows better how to treat such kinds of addicted people. Sooner or later, the day will come it will teach you a good lesson. It has already taught many people in the past.

### 1.2 Gossips and Opinions

In the financial world, we come across various kinds of gossip and opinions. In today's internet age this opinion spreads fast, in our offices, in our homes & everywhere. Online media plays an active role in spreading this opinion and it spreads rapidly with thousands of people. You should not be too attracted by this free advice that is available everywhere. If thousands of people are believing the same thing it doesn't mean that they are always right. Most people have a herd mentality. They discuss only the hot topics that newspapers and media present.

This does not mean that you should stay away from such surroundings. Better, use all this information to arrive at a more logical conclusion. Analyze all available inputs, what they have said, and exactly what has happened. After few exercises, you may be surprised that how this information helps you to make more sound decisions.

I remember the days of 2007; the stock of a company was rising every day. After a few days, its performance was a topic of discussion among people and they started taking interest in it. Some of them were skeptical of this uptrend but the prices did not come down. People became so bullish that they started taking naked positions in futures and options. At the end of the day, they used to get overjoyed and start spreading their opinion about such stocks. But after a few months, at the onset of 2008 when the prices started coming down people didn't get a chance to exit and the prices still haven't come back.

When everything is looking good and making money becomes easy, it is advisable to be cautious. It is good to take a pause when you are in a dilemma. Never forget that you alone are responsible for all matters relating to your money.

## 1.3 Hot Tips

Again, the temptation for making quick money comes here. When we get any advice of hot tips it is very difficult for the person to avoid such kind of temptation and when the informing person says that the news is coming from authentic sources then our greed arouses. Even we do not know from which authentic source it is coming but such kind of information circulates in the market.

People are always happy that they have something more, which others do not have and they feel very proud of having all such information which is coming from unknown sources. Our mind is so fragile that immediately we believe all such information is true and decide to put our money without asking a single question.

People are in a hurry to become millionaires the next day and they feel that the stock market is the shortest way to fulfill their dreams. But what is the outcome of all such transactions, which you have done without putting a single thought on your mind; only losses. The profitability of these hot tips is almost nil and if you can make money in some cases then it will arouse your greed and later it will put you into a major financial crisis.

There are various kinds of people in the market who use all such channels to spread the information for their benefit. If more and more buyers will come then prices will move up. So, they are interested to spread the information, and everyone has a belief that they have something more than others.

These unknown persons also spread erroneous news in the market for their benefit. In today's era, this freely available information has great power to influence the mind of the people. These unknown persons know better when to enter in the stock and when to exit. But many investors are not aware and they get caught in the greed of earning quick money.

When I came across such kinds of hot tips in my career, I found few things are common among them, like;

- The future of these companies is very bright
- Soon, this small-cap will become a mid-cap stock and this mid-cap will become a large-cap stock
- Soon, the company is about to turnaround

- Soon, a white knight is secretly planning to enter this stock

And one of the most amazing things is that – "No one knows this information other than you". What a pity! But people are ready to believe it.

Every action on your 'Hot Tips' stops your mind to think independently.

### 1.4 Expert's Advice: Put A Question Mark

Whenever the market is volatile, people are looking for justification for the price fluctuations. Financial journalists call the market experts to know their opinion about the market. Either they come up with a viable explanation or refuse to be oblivious to the events. People feel comfortable with rational justification. Therefore, every expert prepares himself for all logical reasons before going to the media, so that the public can be convinced.

We must not forget that every person has his prejudice and experts are not untouched by it. They know that the media is providing an opportunity to talk to thousands of people. So, consciously or unconsciously his statement may be coloured by his personal biases.

For example, if the market is falling and journalists ask an expert for his opinion about the current downtrend, and the expert does not want the market to fall further. Therefore, they shall make such statements;

- Don't worry, this fall is temporary
- Investors need not be panic, the market will bounce soon, etc.

However, it may be possible that inside he wants the market not to fall further. So, he will provide all such statements only related to stabilization in the market. There may be a possibility that he says so unconsciously, but statements given on public platforms are linked to personal biases and no expert remains untouched by it.

What does it mean?

It means that you need to understand how all this quickly and freely available information works and as an investor you should know how it affects and unnecessarily shouldn't pay attention to the opinions of others. If the opinion of an expert goes against your opinion, then you should not let yourself be distracted.

## 1.5 You Have Missed the Opportunity

The stock market offers plenty of investment opportunities in good and quality stocks. So, if someone will say that this is a once-in-a-lifetime opportunity, it is better to skip that opportunity. Do not follow such advice, as everyone in this market is looking for their advantage. You must raise a question that why has this person suddenly become such a well-wisher to me, who has never asked for a cup of tea before.

Various untruthful persons want to spread false news in the market and many people start believing in it. For them, every authenticity of news is price movement in stocks.

Prices are going up does not mean that it is a good stock and prices are going down does not mean that it is a bad stock. Without fundamentals, if the prices have gone down it will not come back, and if you fall into a trap in any speculative stock then soon it will become junk.

The arguments of these unscrupulous persons for investing in such speculative stocks are very immature;

- If the news is not true then why are the share prices rising?
- If you're not buying, you're missing out on a good opportunity.
- Look what happened to me, I bought it just a few days ago and I made a lot of money in this stock.
- Investing principles don't work in the real world, you have to act fast.

Many investors fall into a trap on such kind of advice and they enter when the stock is trading at the top. When the investors enter on a belief of such kind of free friendship information, they find that suddenly heavy selling started. They fall into a trap, and their advisor of this free friendship suddenly disappears.

Get rid of all these free friendship advisors, who say if you will not act on this advice, you will miss the opportunity.

### 1.6 Do Not Blame Others

On the belief of others, you cannot remain invested in any stock for the long term. Stock analysis demands your intelligence. Therefore, many investors want to put such a burden on the shoulders of others. They don't want to analyze the facts and figures but want to enjoy the fruit. Therefore, such kinds of questions are very familiar in the stock market –

- Where to invest?
- Which stock is looking good?
- Which one is the next multi-bagger?

If you have not done any analysis and decided to put your money, then do not blame others if your investment has gone wrong. People want to reap the fruit of other's intelligence but are also ready to blame if anything goes wrong.

Better, you can take the input from others, analyze the facts and figures, do your research and then put your money only when you are convinced. You must have logical reasoning in your selected stock. Many people only follow what is prevalent because they cannot see beyond the curtains. Many of them don't believe in their decisions, they don't want to do hard work to find the stuff for research and analysis, they don't want to apply their mind and want to remain protected in their shell.

Therefore, they look for others' intelligence and are ready to blame too if their investment does not fructify.

Belief in yourself is the key to investment success. Independent thinking means whatever will happen I am the responsible person and I believe in my decision.

## Key Points

- Always avoid hot impulses of any kind.
- Freely available information has strong power to influence our decision-making process. You should not rush to invest that you are going to miss the opportunity.
- Don't blame others if you haven't done any analysis and decided to invest your money.
- The key to success in investing is believing in yourself.

## *Chapter 2*

# Influence, Prejudices, and Barriers

When it comes to the matter of money the psychological factors affect us strongly than any other matter. In every movement of price, there is an emotion involved. Consciously or unconsciously, every investor is influenced by many internal and external forces that have strong power to affect their decisions. Electronic media, news, information from surroundings, gossips, etc., all these factors have strong power to influence us seriously, as discussed earlier.

One of the greatest weaknesses of the human mind is, it wants everything right now and quickly, the mind doesn't like to wait for anything. Therefore, when the chance of making money comes in front of an investor, by way of any news or information in stocks, etc. their mind wants to encash it quickly. It is easily influenced by these forces because it doesn't want to lose the opportunity. The mind wants to get results soon because it doesn't like to wait. But, when you act quickly, you can overlook a lot of important things and your chances of making the right decision become minimal.

Greed and fear are the two extreme factors between which our mind swings. When any negative news spread in the market, the mind wants to take action fast, it wants to get rid of this imminent danger quickly and jump on a safe place immediately. Without asking a single question, is there a danger or is it only a rumour, people want to jump from there. Because their mind says to take action quickly, otherwise you would be late. That is the reason rumour matters in the market.

## 2.1 A Balanced Mind

A rational thinking person does not take any impulsive action after hearing news from any source. A successful investor tries to keep his balance of mind and instead of taking any quick action, he says that it is better to first know what the risk is, does it exist or just an illusion. He will take action only when a real danger signal is present.

His mind does not fluctuate with information coming on mobile, television flashes or market rumours, etc. A balanced mind is an asset of a person and your every act influence it.

- If you take quick action on every meagre or trivial information then you are far away from a properly balanced mind.
- If you feel panic after getting some worthless information because that is related to your stake, then you are going in the opposite direction with a balanced mind.
- If you are not able to control your mind over such trivial information and feel panic, then how will you control when suddenly you have a flood of information.

When panic selling occurs in the market many investors want to sell everything without properly analyzing what type of news has come and what is its long-term impact. This is because they are losing their mental balance and want to see results quickly. Their mind is not ready for such type of scenarios, because these types of incidents seldom happen in the market and they want to keep safe their investment quickly without proper understanding of the danger.

You must have a properly balanced mind to take right and timely decisions. You would be able to overcome the influence of internal and external factors if your mind is strong enough to face such forces. You cannot achieve this in a day or two; it is a journey and every day you have to learn to balance your mind.

## 2.2 Prejudices

Each personality is different and has its own biases as they have different experiences in life. The person who is deceived by those close to him has his own prejudices and is very cautious and fearful when making a decision next time, while another whose life is on the easy path is less likely to be so cautious. Your prejudices restrict you to move in a certain direction because your mind is not ready for that.

When a negative news outbreak in the market many investors start selling their shares as they have their prejudice to secure their money, but an astute investor who has a proper understanding of news is waiting for such kind of incident in the market to enter in quality stocks.

When prices start dropping fearful investors start feeling panic because they have not done in-depth analysis so they want to exit it soon, but a confident investor who has patience, carefully wait for the right movement to enter the market. This is the reason that after some fall in the market, buying support emerges and after some time gradually the market starts stabilizing.

Every investor follows a certain behaviour and many times this behaviour creates obstacles that prevent from achieving the goal and due to this characteristic people take a wrong decision and realize it later.

When the market is hitting new highs every day and everything is booming, the excitement among the market participants is clearly visible. The stock market works on probability but without proper understanding, people believe that buoyancy will continue forever and it is a good time to make hay while the sun shines. They make decisions as per their prejudices but believe that they are away from all this.

## 2.3 Repeating the Same Mistake

We know the old phrase - “To err is human”. But what about those who make the same mistake over and over again. Many of them have lost money several times in trading activity but again eager to come back and take positions. Many people learn from the mistakes of others but many of them are not even ready to learn from their own mistakes. It seems that they are not ready to learn from their own mistakes. Making the same mistake over and over again is a big obstacle that hinders your learning.

What is the psychology behind making the same mistake over and over again, because if it is a mistake and the person knows, he should not do it again?

If you become humble and accept that ‘Yes’ this is the mistake and I have done it, then you will not do it again. Only a fool is ready to burn his fingers of doing the same fallacious things repeatedly. But ego is more important which prevents the person to become humble. Due to this ego, such type of person is not ready to accept that it was a mistake and they have done it. Their ego says you have taken a right decision and whatever rest has happened that is due to this reason and due to that reason...etc. They are more interested in protecting their ego than in learning. They keep protecting it in every incident and gradually the balloon of ego gets inflated in their mind. Such people learn in their life only when there is a big setback, when the balloon of ego bursts.

### 2.4 Personal Attachment

Many people have a personal attachment to the organization they work for over the years. It takes years to build strong pillars and these people worked hard to make such pillars for the organization. Many times, the new recruits do not even know what sacrifices the old generation has made to make such a strong pillar in the organization. But the ageing generation has only one objective, they want to keep their money safe for retirement. Therefore, the personal attachment to the organization is less in the newcomers and more in the older people.

Sometimes, because of this belief, older people accumulate too much stock in the company they work for years, thinking that all these investments are for their retirement. They forget that due to such activity the overall weightage of their portfolio has become unbalanced. Because of their personal feeling, they take interest in investing a huge amount of money in only one stock but they forget to remember that money has no emotion.

Such action diminishes the benefits of diversification and increases the risk of placing all the eggs in only one basket. Personal attachment to any company is another barrier that prevents from making a proper decision.

## 2.5 Choose Your Investment Style

Every mind is different therefore it is good to choose your investment style. Someone's mind is better to understand investment for long-term, someone's mind is better to understand trading calls, someone's mind is better to understand futures and options, etc. It is good to analyze your personality first and act only on what you can understand better. Do not copy the path of others. You can follow the theme but the style must be yours.

"Imitation is the surest form of flattery and failure."

- Miyamoto Musashi

**Key Points**

- A properly balanced mind is required to take right and timely decisions.
- Sometimes your prejudices create barriers that prevent you from achieving your goals. People make decisions according to their prejudices but believe that they are far from it.
- Personal attachment to any company is a hindrance that prevents proper decision making.
- Choose your own investment style that best suits your personality.

## Chapter 3

# Reluctance and Assurance

When people find something new that they are not very comfortable with, they feel reluctant. They want to protect themselves from these unknown consequences, but when they see that there is an element of security involved, they gradually overcome their reluctance and reassurance begins to come upon new things.

In the same way, when people are walking alone on the road which they are not aware of, they feel reluctant but when they come to know that hundreds and thousands of men are also walking on the same path, they feel reassured.

In the matter of investment, people first look for assurance. They are looking for safety while following the path of others. Their mind says that many people cannot make wrong decisions at the same time. So, when their reluctance gradually turns into assurance, they follow the same path. With the idea of keeping their investments safe, many people follow the investments made by others without any analysis. Behavioural finance refers to this type of mindset as the herd mentality.

In today's electronic world, media plays a vital role in increasing the level of assurance among the people. When people start looking at the same information here and there, their reassurance starts coming and the fear of reluctance gradually dissipates. When assurance comes, they feel that there is no need to analyze further, because assurance brings trust, and that matters.

### 3.1 Be Reluctant

Without doing your research on the belief of others, if you convert your reluctance into assurance then you may put yourself in trouble. When you are going to invest your money in an investment product that you are not aware of and have not done any analysis, be reluctant at first. Investing your money in any investment product, even if millions of people have already invested, is like traveling alone in the ocean where no one will come to the rescue if your decision is wrong. Therefore, it is good to convert your reluctance into assurance only on your belief and not on the belief of others.

Sometimes you will find that it is very difficult to decide under certain circumstances. When a person is reluctant to make his investment, but the environment forces him to act quickly and he does not have the proper time to do any research in all this. In such circumstances, go through all the information available so far and take a tea break before taking any action.

Contemplate all the information and try to pacify all your thoughts, when the waves are calm, the surface is clearly visible, now you can see deep down to the bottom. Most people make wrong decisions when their mind waves are too impulsive and they jump into action without calming those thoughts down. Because once you take a step forward it is very difficult to come back.

## 3.2 Choose Your Initial Steps Carefully

As discussed in the previous chapter, the weakness of the human mind is that it is always looking for quick action, so even those who do not have good intentions want to turn the other person's reluctance into assurances for their quick gains. First, they send some advice for very attractive investments and then immediately call you looking for assurance. When they find that this is not enough, they send you some more information and seek your reassurance, and keep doing so until your final assurance comes.

When you observe all these situations you will realize that an impulse is involved in all these processes because the mind doesn't want to wait.

When such mischievous people think that their potential investor is taking too much time, they become impatient, their mind becomes reckless because they want to see the results quickly. They will make every effort to catch you and you will find one behaviour that is common with all these acts and that is they want to see results quickly.

In these circumstances, this type of impulsivity provides a clear indication of being reluctant to take the first step, dig deeper to find out the truth, because taking the second step could be costly for you.

Moving in any direction requires time and energy and each individual has a limited amount of time and energy. Therefore, before starting your journey in any direction it is necessary to analyze all facts and figures and choose your first few steps very carefully.

Your steps decide your destination which you have not yet seen and after a long journey you will reach there but your steps in the initial stages have already determined it.

### Key Points

- Do not put your money on belief of others, do your own analysis.
- Do not take hasty decisions, if quick action requires it is good to imbibe all available information and pacify all the waves of mind before taking any action.
- Sometimes, taking a second step in a direction can be costly, so it's good to hold off on the first step if your initial observation doesn't support moving forward.
- Remember, your initial steps decide your destination.

## Chapter 4

# Childish Mentality: Get Rid of it Before Investing

We all go through different stages of life; childhood, adult, and old age. As we enter our youth, we start making financial decisions. People become interested in stocks and other avenues of investment. As time passes, they become a mature person but many of them never think that there is still a child in their mind that influences their decisions. Many people stock buying decisions influenced by their childish mindset. Due to this mindset, they have to suffer many times. They want to get rich quickly but after a few incidents, they leave the market forever.

I have noticed the following emotional immaturity when buying stocks by various investors:

### 4.1 Large Quantity

**Child Behaviour:** *Children like to have a large number of toffees and chocolates in their pockets. They are not satisfied by taking only one or two pieces. Even they are unable to eat but they want to keep it in their pocket and they feel very happy keeping it in their pocket.*

**Adult Behaviour:** *While adults do not take interest in such types of activities.*

Many investors have a similar mindset when considering buying a stock. They are always interested in ultra-cheap penny stocks or shares that they can hoard in bulk quantities without properly understanding the fundamentals of the company.

First, they look at the price and mentally calculate the quantity they can buy, and if the quantity comes down, they ignore all the fundamentals, all the stock advice, not even ready to pay attention. What matters most for them is quantity. The same childish mindset that wants to have more toffees and chocolates in their pockets. I have noticed that many investors have only those stocks in their portfolios that they can accumulate large amounts of. Even though all the fundamentals of these stocks are gone, they retain it for years. Holding a big quantity of stocks in their portfolio satisfying the childish mentality that they have a large number of toffies and chocolates in their pockets although there is no meaning of that.

### 4.2 Emotional Vicissitudes

**Child Behaviour:** *Children often cry and please very easily.*

**Adult Behaviour:** *Adults seldom do.*

This is the behaviour I have seen among many investors. When prices drop below their purchase price, they immediately feel panic and start collecting information from their sources to confirm that their money is safe. When prices jump up immediately, they are happy and rush to make a quick profit.

### 4.3 Impulsive Behaviour

**Child Behaviour:** *Children are impulsive, they speak casually, they do not want to wait for anything, they act impulsively without thinking about the possible consequences.*

**Adult Behaviour:** *Adults tend to calm themselves down, gather more information before taking any action.*

I found this behaviour among many investors. For example, when someone gets a call that the price of a stock is going up, some people decide to take immediate action without a second thought, without examining the fundamentals of the company, whether that information is accurate or not. Impulsive behaviour prompts them to take action without thinking about the possible consequences that are likely to occur if the said information is not correct.

### 4.4 Blaming Someone Else

**Child Behaviour:** *Children tend to blame others when anything goes wrong.*

**Adult Behaviour:** *Adults try to identify the problem and find solutions.*

When investors buy stocks on the recommendation of others and prices start falling, they immediately start blaming others. Where as a mature investor tries to identify the reason for the fall in price and then decides whether it is a buying opportunity or something has gone wrong in the company.

*(Also discussed in Chapter 1: Independent Thinking)*

### 4.5 Unable to Face Reality

**Child Behaviour:** *Sometimes children lie to avoid trouble.*

**Adult Behaviour:** *While grown-ups are ready to face reality.*

When markets are performing better, many investors invest borrowed money in the stock market. Sometimes they make money and later many starts gambling. When anything goes wrong, they try to hide such information from their family and friends. They are not ready to admit their mistakes start speaking untruth and try to avoid themselves from that situation. They still haven't grown up to face reality.

### 4.6 Comfort Zone

**Child Behaviour:** *Children are incapable of taking risks and they are always looking for safety and comfort zones.*

**Adult Behaviour:** *They are ready to face challenges.*

Many investors feel the safety and comfort zone when they come to know that their friends have bought the same stock or some big name associated with the stock market has also bought the same. Then they feel the security of their money. Without knowing what are the products and services of this company or without doing any research of the company, they decide to buy a large amount of stock. The comfort zone is one of the biggest hurdles for an investor. To break the barrier, you have to do your research.

### 4.7 Self-Admiration

**Child Behaviour:** *Children want everyone to listen to them. They feel great appreciation when the elders of their family listen attentively to their great work and they keep saying it again and again among others.*

**Adult Behaviour:** *While psychologically strong people like to listen to others.*

The same behaviour I observed among many investors when they book profit in any stock. They start saying that how smart they are, how they book profits.

Tendency to self-praise and the same childish mentality of narrating the events around you.

Rather than admiring their small successes here and there, psychologically strong people utilize the time for their bigger goals.

### The Bottom Line

It is difficult for many investors to let go of the childish mindset. We all learn from our mistakes but if you stick to the childhood mindset then you will never learn from your mistakes. Children's thinking is shallow, they cannot go deep because their mind is not yet developed. Your childish mentality will not allow you to go in deep if you will trumpet your small success of stocks here and there. Because you have not gone deep, repetition of success will be difficult, soon you may have to suffer loss. Just as our body requires food, so is the nourishment of the mind through good education.

## Key Points

Following are the important childish mindset that seriously impacts while taking the financial decisions;

- Investing in ultra-cheap penny stocks in bulk quantities without properly understanding the fundamentals of the company.
- Feeling immediate panic, when prices drop below their buying price.
- Taking prompt action without thinking about the possible consequences.
- Unable to face reality, when financial decisions go wrong, etc.

## Chapter 5

# Contrary Opinion

- *What is a contrary opinion?*
- *Why is an investor unwilling to follow the path chosen by the crowd?*
- *Why does their mind compel them not to go ahead with the masses?*
- *Under what circumstances a contrarian thinker believes that when most investors are heading towards a certain direction, the time has come to jump from there.*

Before discussing all these points, we need to know how our brain functions.

We adopt the language, culture and dress of the place where we are born, because our senses are constantly affected by all these things, gradually, we become accustomed and our mind accept them very easily.

The same principle works for many people when it comes to investing. When investors see that the majority of people around them are buying or selling a particular stock or any other investment product, they tend to think of doing the same. But the matter of investment is not as easy. It requires understanding of the company, industry, economy, etc. History tells us that most people have a herd mentality and they follow only what they see in their surroundings.

But some investors are not ready to follow that path, where others are going, they tend to be the contrarian thinkers.

Emotions play an essential role while taking decisions and the matter of money is always related to our emotions. When a large number of people are thinking in the same direction then emotions rule. In such conditions, reasons and logical thinking becomes immaterial and many of them start flowing in the same direction as the wind of emotions flows.

Understanding crowd psychology is very important before taking a contrary opinion. If you want to keep yourself aloof, you must have a strong understanding of the behaviour of the masses. Masses flow with emotions and where emotions matter, reasoning fails. You should create a mechanism for yourself that helps to take decisive decisions, that helps you to create a strong mind. Your mind should not flow with emotions. It should not distract with hot impulses.

### 5.1 Contrarian Thinker

In the financial world, these emotions are like bubbles that start accumulating air of making easy money and slowly become bigger and bigger. Gradually, people start thinking that making money in this route is very easy and every day the temptation becomes more when they start seeing results in the surrounding environment. As time passes, various types of people who are not aware of this kind of field start entering this easy money-making business, and the creation of a big bubble starts.

But the mind of a contrarian thinker works differently. Rather than jumping into such flow, the contrarian thinker starts thinking – 'Is this the creation of a bubble'. He starts watching the behaviour of the masses, analyzing the financial data, collecting information about historical bubbles, and study how they got busted. With knowledge and experience, he understands that the time has come to take a contrarian call. It is true that history repeats, but will not repeat in the same way. Never two market bubbles are the same.

During the boom of 2007, many people were thinking that making money in the stock market is very easy, and without thinking they started jumping in that direction which they had no idea about. They started playing in the stock market with their savings and personal investments. That time everybody had a stock tip, and at the end of the day cheer on their faces was clearly visible. Not only educated people, but even working-class people of the society who have no understanding about industry and economy also started recommending stocks. Small-shop owners, taxi drivers, etc. all had stock tips and they felt very happy when their tips performed better.

During Dotcom Bubble in the late 90s, many people start floating IT companies who do not know how IT company functions. The hunger for easy money had become so high that many people left their jobs to trade in the financial market to become the next day millionaire.

Media plays a very important role in all these scenarios. Many discussions on media start on these hot topics and people start taking very much interest to listen to all this information. A bunch of IPOs starts coming and news of becoming a quick millionaire has become very much fancy.

The local newspapers which never published any news about stocks, industry, and economy, suddenly start taking very much interest. Publishing of articles related to such hot topics become common and many times it became the headlines of these newspapers. The same thing also happens in the case when pessimism spreads in the market.

When such kind of signal occurs that is enough to take a contrary opinion. Do not try to share your opinion with others. No one is ready to listen if you say anything against the crowd.

Carefully observe the behaviour of the masses, listen to the hot discussions and when you realize that many people are easily accepting the absurd outcome, simply hit the sell button.

## 5.2 Before Taking a Contrarian Call

Many investors want to take the opportunity of a contrarian view. Looking to the history that a successful contrarian call provides a big opportunity that rarely occurs in the market, they prefer to take contrarian calls.

One should always remember that always going against the masses is not a contrary opinion. You cannot take such calls blindly. But many people believe that when the majority of the people is thinking in a certain manner, I must think against the crowd.

Some common behaviours I've seen in the market:

- Many people start taking a short position when a stock hit an all-time high / 52 week high

- In the same manner, many of them start accumulating the stock when it is falling, in hope that contrary opinion will reward them high

But the question is before taking such types of contrarian call, whether you have a strong logic or not for the position you are going to create. If you don't have a proper understanding of the fundamentals, '*I'm a contrarian thinker*', would only be a fancy word for you, and if you act on it, you'll make a wrong decision.

In case of heavy selling in the market on a certain stock, many investors start accumulating it without knowing the reason that what suddenly has happened or when a stock is available at a very cheap price, then they start bottom fishing on the thought of that I am a contrarian thinker.

For whatever be the reason, when the selling pressure is high, it is just like a falling knife. In such circumstances, it is good to wait for sometime to stabilize the situation.

*But the question is how do we know that stabilization has come.*

When a knife is falling from the top and heading towards the bottom its momentum is high, but when it touches the ground, its momentum stops. In the same manner, when a stock is falling from the top its momentum is high. I have seen that when a stock is falling and in a single day, fall is 8% to 10% or even more, that time it is not good to take a contrarian call. Wait for stabilization, there is a possibility that for the next few days the fall may continue. After sometime, it hits the bottom and the fall is reduced to less than 5%, then less than 2% and the stock starts forming a zig-zag pattern. The knife has reached the bottom now you can safely pick it up.

You should not be in a hurry to jump in such kind of stock on a thought that I am a contrarian thinker. If you have not waited for stabilization and if you do not have a sound reason to enter, such kind of contrary opinion will be costly for you.

For example, when the stock of a leading bank was falling and when it falls below rupees 100, many investors started accumulating the stock on the thought of being contrary in the market. When it falls below rupees 50, they started doing averages.

Lack of proper knowledge and blindly taking a contrarian call may cost you high. Accumulation of stocks when prices are falling is not a contrary opinion. Your logic must be very strong for investment before taking a contrary opinion and this you will learn through enhancing your knowledge and enriching your experience.

### 5.3 When Everyone is Expecting the Same

The contrary opinion is the art of understanding the psychology of the masses rather than just dealing with financial numbers. Many investors make their decisions based on the financial numbers that are readily available nowadays. Based on these numbers they take a call and expect that the market will behave in a certain way. When everyone is expecting the same thing, the probability of the occurrence of the event becomes minimal.

For example, when everyone expects that market will fall from here, but it does not fall. Because in this market along with numbers, emotions also matter.

Therefore, many times you will find that logic always does not work in the market.

It is demanding something more from you and that is to understand the psychology of the masses.

### 5.4 Trend is Your Friend, but Not Always

A novice trader always follows the old maxim – "Trend is your Friend". It is also true that the level of saturation will also come after a certain time. This may be possible on either side, up or down. When the market is rising, exuberance is bullish, and when it is falling pessimism spreads. Under such circumstances, taking a contrarian call requires solid analysis which is very difficult for the person who has less experience in the market. Also, it is very difficult to catch the trend reversal, because the sentiment of the masses does not vanish overnight.

For example, suppose negative news has come in the market, and stocks starts taking a dip. The news is in front of many investors but every person has a different opinion. Every investor does not feel optimism and pessimism at the same time. Not everyone may have the same opinion about a related event.

I remember the day in January 2008, when indices start falling, even then people were very optimistic and they use every dip for the accumulation of the stocks. The boom in the market that they have seen from the past, their mind is not ready to leave easily. The sentiments which are coming from the past, suddenly cannot take a U-turn. Human sentiments are like waves, gradually it comes and gradually it goes.

We are not prepared to do a solid analysis of the news when we internally want the market not to fall from here. We keep our emotions on top of the news, and prefer to sit in a comfortable zone that everything is fine, there is no need to worry.

A *danger exists only where when we feel that we are in a comfortable zone.*

While taking a contrary opinion you are going to take a decision which is totally against the current market trend. Therefore, your decision should not be based on only one factor. You have to analyze it with fundamentals, technicals and also understand the involved human emotions.

## 5.5 Momentum and Demand

The upside momentum in the stock should be supported by the increase in demand of its shares and vice versa. But what happens when demand is decreasing and the upside momentum is continuing or demand is increasing but there is no momentum. When such a situation occurs in the market, a contrarian thinker carefully analyzes the relationship between these two factors, i.e., momentum and demand.

If the uptrend is not supported by the demand of its shares, then survival for such kinds of stocks at the top is very difficult. Soon, speculators exit, and prices start taking a dip. But in such conditions, many investors start accumulating the stock because they think that such a high valued stock is now available at very attractive valuations and soon it will cross its previous high. But they forget that demand is waning and soon if the fundamentals of the company does not change then their investment will go into jeopardy.

If the stock is hitting 52 week high/all-time high, do not take a contrarian call before looking at the demand for its products. If you find that there is no sign of a decrease in demand then don't go against the momentum.

Stocks that have strong demand for their products never come down even after hitting 52-week highs/all-time highs. These stocks have given tremendous returns over the long term and have seen no downside except the market downturn. Stocks like Bata India, Britannia, Bajaj Finance, etc. have been able to outperform over the past few years due to increased demand for their products.

The contrary opinion requires a lot of knowledge and experience in the market. It is not for immature persons to take such important decisions. But immature persons have opinions like that;

- I am going against the crowd
- The crowd is always wrong
- Do the opposite of what others are doing, etc.

Such types of thinkers are not contrarians. Due to their audacious personality, they simply want to enjoy going against the crowd.

Contrarian thinkers do not take the advice of others. To take such tough decisions contrarian's minds are so strong and suited to investment methodology, that it is not ready to follow the absurdness of the masses.

## Key Points

- Masses flow with emotions and where emotions matter, reasoning fails.
- Contrarian thinkers are not ready to follow the path of masses, their mind works differently.
- A danger exists only where when we feel that we are in a comfortable zone.
- To take a contrary call requires a lot of knowledge and experience in the market, it is not for immatures.
- Contrarian thinkers do not take the advice of others and their mind is not ready to follow the absurdness of masses.

*Chapter - 6*

# Depression

A feeling of anxiety is normal about something for the time being, but if such feeling lasts for a longer time which affects the mental and physical health of the person, then it is not common and it may be a symptom of depression. Whether the matter is related to money or something else but it means that something has happened or is happening in a person's life that he does not want and the circumstances is putting him under deep pressure. A sudden loss of money or a sudden shock of some unforeseen event seriously affects the mental health of the person.

## 6.1 A Sudden Loss of Wealth

Trade in the stock market works on probability. When the reward potential is greater than the associated risk, it is called a favourable trade. The improper decision of risk-reward ratio can put a person in deep trouble. Choosing the wrong stock for investment that spoils the wealth of investors or a sudden market crash can put a person under severe mental stress or depression.

Under these circumstances, the mind of a person is not prepared to face such a situation. He wants to come out of that situation somehow but nothing is working. Gradually a lot of negative thoughts start coming and those thoughts put the person under deep pressure that he is not ready to bear. When the situation goes from bad to worse, the person starts keeping himself in isolation. Deteriorating mental health can put a person in distress and lead to frustration, loneliness, hopelessness, loss of interest and appetite, withdrawal from social contacts, and more negative thoughts about the future.

Gradually the person starts losing confidence, his energy level starts decreasing, the problem of insomnia starts due to the constant flow of negative thoughts as he starts feeling that the situation has entangled him, whatever is happening that will last forever and there is no way to get rid of the situation, he finds himself a victim of circumstances that he cannot change.

Remember that no cycle in the market remains constant. Fluctuations are part of the market and are inevitable. Don't take hasty decisions and go through all the past decisions taken by you carefully. The time is demanding to throw all the useless information out of your mind.

## 6.2 Failure - Enrichment of Experience

Except for a few lucky ones, not everything in your life goes the way you want it to be. Sometimes circumstances force a person to change the chosen path, which he is afraid to go because he does not know in which direction the path is going and what will be its destination. Your mind says that you have already wasted so much time and energy through so many different paths, achieved nothing, why should you refocus your energy in those directions where the destination is unknown.

In such circumstances due to the ambiguity of direction and lack of enthusiasm one finds himself that his mind is not ready to put energy, and where there is no energy, there will be no result.

On the other hand, if you analyze the positive outcome of this journey, you will realize that failure from other directions is not failure, it enriches your experience. You are now aware of the difficult situations you didn't already know about and decided to jump in due to insufficient knowledge. Now you have crossed a level to become an experienced person/a master. During this journey, you got a vision and now you can say with confidence that what you should do and what you should not do. At the onset of the journey, you were an immature person but now you are not the same person who started the journey.

In the beginning, you thought that the path you have chosen will bring you success. With great enthusiasm and with full energy you entered on that path and burnt your fingers. Now you are aware of the difficulties, shortcomings, real and false attractions, etc.

It is good to say, now you have seen the real picture;

- Now your vision is not blurred, you got a penetrating vision, which many persons do not have
- Now you are fully aware of the naked truth and with such awareness, you are not going to do the same mistake again

So, instead of saying failure on such situations in life, I would like to say– "The person has elevated himself to the next level of maturity."

The matter of investing is all about the precision of your thinking and your decision will be correct only when you have enough courage to take it and accept full responsibility for the consequences. It is an art and one learns from experiences in life.

### 6.3 Big Expectations

People feel depressed not because they have failed in a particular direction, but because they have high expectations before going down that path and there is a high assurance of success in that direction.

When the deviation occurs on the chosen path, their mind is not ready for that and they find themselves in a perplexing situation. But when the circumstances forced them to change the track, they find themselves in a state of complete darkness. All expectations about their dreamland suddenly disappear. Their mind is not ready to face such a setback, as the mind is already on some other path, so how is it possible to change the track quickly?

Loss of big money in the stock market or failure of a business is such a kind of shock, which many people find difficult to bear. Suddenly they find themselves on the path of complete darkness. Circumstances are forcing them to change the track but their mind is not ready to absorb it and they put themselves in a state of depression. Life is teaching them a new lesson but the mind is not ready to accept it.

What you lost in these circumstances; money, business, or something else. In my opinion, the person has lost his energy, he lost his self-confidence. That is why he has surrounded himself in a state of darkness.

I have seen that the problem of depression is more related to high expectations. Many people enter the stock market with the expectations that they will make big money soon, and their confidence starts building up after some successes. Without any knowledge of the industry, economy, and fundamentals of the company, they start taking big trade positions in the market. But after some time, suffering from major losses, they leave the market forever. After such circumstances, many of them find themselves the victim of depression.

Without proper understanding of the chosen path, you will land yourself in deep trouble if you go ahead with such high expectations.

Many people start looking for different shortcuts in the stock market because the lure of making big money immediately attracts them towards it. Because their knowledge is very superficial about the subject, many unscrupulous people start showing them the way how to get big money quickly and easily, and then their mind says 'Yes' this is the path I was looking for and due to your greed, you can be ready to follow it. Many people lost their big money in the stock market because they are looking for shortcuts.

I observed some identifications of such kind of mischievous persons that till the attainment of their task;

- They will never say anything which will go against you
- Which may hurt you or act anything which can be harmful to you
- Sometimes they praise you in front of others for no reason of how talented you are
- They offer you their help in every matter of life and sometimes blames you why you didn't inform him about a problem that he can solve very quickly

Such double-faced people always say and behave differently, only doing things that you will find believable, because their goal is to increase your trust in them every day. Gradually, your vision of looking beyond the curtains becomes blurry and your balloon of hope gets bigger and bigger every day.

What mistakes the person is doing in these circumstances;

- He is looking for shortcuts
- He is looking for quick success
- He is more interested in money matters, not the learning process

I noticed that such people who look for shortcuts are not interested in increasing their knowledge. They prefer money-related discussions rather than spending time to hone their skills or to learn new skills, and such discussions give them a sense of joy.

Balloons are only good for children's play and decorations. A balloon is not designed to withstand a small pin or heat. Similarly, the balloon of hope in your mind bursts when you face the real heat/challenges of life. In such a situation, the circumstances put the person in pain, frustration, and depression.

## 6.4 Unsuccessful Attempts Brings Closer to Success

We all know the famous invention of the electric bulb by Thomas Alva Edison. As an inventor, Edison made 1,000 unsuccessful attempts at inventing the light bulb. He never frustrates with doing one more research the next day. He used to say that the unsuccessful attempts bring him closer to success. When a reporter asked, "How did it feel to fail 1,000 times?" Edison replied, "I didn't fail 1,000 times. The light bulb was an invention with 1,000 steps."

But many people are not ready to accept the failure in just one attempt. They want success very quickly and easily, and every small success immediately pulls their expectations on a very high level. After doing few efforts if the person is not getting success, then immediately, they start feeling depressed.

Have you ever thought, what will happen if you get success very easily?

It is like you reach the top of the building with the help of a lift or you reach the top of the mountain with the help of a helicopter/airplane.

Then, there is a strong possibility that you will not be able to digest what you have achieved money, success, fame, etc. If you are not able to digest it then the possibility of losing it is very high.

Like the brain of a child is not developed to understand complex mathematics, but when the child grows and becomes an adult, he understands it easily. In between, what has happened during these years. The child's brain has developed, and now he is ready to understand and digest complex things easily. In the same manner, a person who has taken a lift to reach the top, his brain is not developed. His brain has not done those exercises which are necessary for its development.

I observed such a kind of person very carefully and found that the mindset of children has not yet gone from their mind;

- Such kind of person still has anger like a child on any small issue.
- Sometimes the child demands very strange things from their parents. Demand is also sometimes very strange for these kinds of people.
- Children want to fulfill their demands immediately. Such kind of person also want to fulfill their demand immediately.

- If you say 'no' to kids, they get angry. Such people also do not like to hear 'no'.
- Children cannot accept the denial of their demand and start crying immediately. Such a person also cannot accept any kind of denial. Instead of crying, they get ready to retaliate.
- The stubbornness of the child still remains with the ego of getting the position.
- Childlike self-appreciation listening behaviour is still present, so they are surrounded by people who have nothing to do but praise them.
- Logic doesn't work for the children's minds; logic also doesn't work for these types of people.

Because they have not done their journey towards the top of the mountain, they are unaware of the challenges that exist at each step.

In different circumstances, every day our life produces new challenges. But such kind of person lacks the required skills which are necessary for taking vital decisions. Because they have not taken steps on the path so they are unaware of the reality.

But challenges demand solutions. If their mind is not ready to give any solution then someone else will come to answer. Difficult situations demand real solutions, and the gap for solution should not be long. When circumstances demand to fill the gap and if you do not do so, the chances of the structure collapsing are high.

*Real challenges of life demand real solutions without any imitations.*

When life demands real answers, a person taking shortcuts is again looking for some lift, because that is the way he has learned in his life. Soon the circumstances will kick them out of the top because other people are working too hard to get there and remember, they haven't taken a lift. Therefore, their level of understanding and maturity is completely different from that of a person reaching the top with the help of an elevator.

A person who has worked hard to achieve success and has not taken any lift has a different level of dignity and maturity. Those immature individuals cannot face these real persons because mature individuals are aware of every step and their minds are developed enough to provide solutions in real-time.

Therefore, when your life pulls you back and forces you to make another attempt, do not feel any frustration, time is demanding you to hone your skills. Your mind will gradually become strong enough to face any challenge of life. As Edison said – “It is providing you a chance to come closer to success”.

When your life is putting you on a tough path take it as an opportunity to learn a new thing which might you already do not know, and later it will help to achieve your desired goal.

Build your confidence by slowly tackling small obstacles. This will lead to an accumulation of confidence which will give you more willpower and make you determined and decisive.

Depression has no meaning in the life of a person who has travelled on these paths. Every day new challenges arise in life and every day they are very happy to face them.

**Key Points**

- Don't make hasty decisions and throw away all the information that has lost its usefulness over time.
- You will put yourself in trouble if you enter any path without proper understanding with high expectations.
- The real challenges of life demand real solutions without any imitation.

# *Chapter-7*

# Risk and Success

- *What is the risk?*
- *Why are people ready to take risks?*

*Risk means moving in a direction where we do not know what the outcome is going to be.*

Many people are always looking for a comfort zone and avoid taking any kind of risk. But many of them are willing to take different kinds of risks because the mundane daily activities seem boring and painful to them. So, they are inclined to move in that direction where the outcome is not already known and they feel happy to do so.

People know that smoking is injurious to health, but they accept it. They know that adventure sports are risky, but they are willing to do so. In the same way, high-speed driving, rock climbing, sky diving, and many other activities are done by people with acceptance.

All these acts related to only one thing – "Danger to life". When the danger to our life exists, our mind receives a feeling of pleasure. Psychologists say, at that moment there is a change of hormone in the brain. Adrenaline is a hormone secreted by the adrenal glands that increase the rate of blood circulation, breathing, and carbohydrate metabolism when one is excited, afraid, or angry.

Dopamine is a type of neurotransmitter, our body releases when we experience some pleasurable events. It plays a vital role in how we feel pleasure. This "Feel good" chemical our brain releases when we eat certain food, smell something good, shopping, do drugs, etc., anything that we enjoy. To get this pleasure again our brain encourages us to repeat the action even though too much doing is not good.

Many of them who want to come out of their daily routine become addicted to it. Psychologists call them an adrenaline junkie. Because now their mind knows this simple trick how to get instant pleasure. Watching horror movies, drinking alcohol, taking drugs, gambling, driving recklessly, getting bored easily, and always looking for a change, etc. are nothing but addiction and easy techniques to get some instant pleasure.

Psychologists observe the behaviour of such risk-takers and they called them sensation-seekers. Such kind of people are willing to take small risks for the sake of getting some sensation.

## 7.1 Financial Risk

Rather than putting life into danger or doing something harmful to the human body, many people start taking a financial risk. Such kind of activities also provides getting some thrill and sensation. For getting this sensation people love to gamble, they like to bet on horse races, sports, every uncertain national and international event, etc. Many of them like to bet on every topic of the discussion among their colleagues and friends. What they are looking for, they are looking for some sensation which can provide some pleasure to their mind.

## 7.2 Sensation-Seeking Traders

In the stock market, traders of some sort are always looking for some hot news and tips or some other way to get some sensation. When prices fluctuate, the sentiment goes along with it. This type of person is interested in seeing the price ticker every minute. Instead of making real money, they enjoy the thrill of price fluctuations.

Such kind of people are not ready to listen to long-term investment advice. They are not interested to put any heed on them. Because there is no thrill on long-term investment. Their mind demands a daily dose of sensation, and the stock market provides the best opportunity to get some thrill with no physical harm to life. No matter, whether stock tips are performed well or not. Whether they gain in trade or suffered losses. Many times, they have to bear the loss but immediately they forget it. Again, they are interested in investing in some other hot tips. Every day they are on the lookout for hot news, whatever it may be. They are sensation-seeking traders and it is very difficult for them to give it up because sensation matters to them.

## 7.3 Risk and Alertness

When you are doing the same thing over and over again, your mind gets used to doing it. While working you can discuss, sing songs, there is no need for alertness as you know everything very well. But what happens when you are walking on the road which you do not know, you can't discuss, you can't sing a song. In these unknown circumstances, your mind can't sleep, now you are alert. The unknown is always a danger and where danger exists, our mind becomes alert.

The path which you have not already walked is always risky. There is a danger that exists on every path which you have not travelled. But the excitement associated with uncertainty attracts. That is the reason people are willing to go to new and unknown places and after returning they are full of energy. They realize that their productivity has been increased.

> On walking the unknown path your mind gets a job – "A job of alertness".

I have never been a mountain walker, but I found the tremendous attraction of mountain climbing among people. The risk of going on the top of the mountain is nothing but the pleasure of alertness. As you are heading towards the top, more and more alertness is required. A single mistake will be costly for you.

In the same manner, for any task where a big risk is involved, you can't do a single mistake. This requires your high alertness.

### 7.4 Success and Alertness

Success demands your alertness. A careless person has a strong possibility to fall on the chosen path. Like a mountain walker can't be careless, so one who seeks success cannot be careless.

The same thing happens while meeting with an unknown person and dealing with them. Your mind is fully alert. It starts analyzing all new situations. Within a limited time frame, you have to analyze a lot of things and it requires full alertness of your mind.

I observed that, for many persons who are in sales and marketing jobs, it is very difficult for them to sit idle at one place. Such kind of people find that their productivity stops if they involve themselves in any sitting job. The feed which requires to activate their mind is now missing. Therefore, they feel lethargic in any other kind of job where there is no momentum.

People are looking for success but they avoid taking any kind of risk. Whole day they watch television and discuss how to get success. For them, success means safe success which can be achieved without taking any kind of risk.

What type of alertness your mind will get when the whole day you are watching television sitting on the sofa and eating snacks? After some time, such kind of people become afraid of anything new and unknown in their life. Because they have trained their mind in such a manner.

Taking risks in small ways that are not addictive is good for mental health. It helps to come out from negative thoughts. Such type of person has a strong capacity to fight against all odds and never accepts any defeat in his life even if the time is not favourable for him.

## 7.5 Fear of Failure

No matter how much analysis you did before taking a risk for getting success, but fear of failure is always there. This fear of failure puts your mind in a high alert zone. When the stake is high, the fear of failure is also high. When chances of failure are high, it requires more alertness of your mind.

At that moment every cell of your body is fully active and your mind is fully alert. When your mind is alert, you observe everything very carefully and you cannot take decisions without thorough considerations. All these require your utmost attention and then the chances of success start coming closer to you.

Whether you are going to choose a new career or going to start a new business, the new path is always risky. The fear of failure is always there and that requires your full attention. The excitement associated with your new venture puts you in such an active state where the pleasure of success is waiting. In such a state of mind, there is no possibility of any boredom, frustration, depression, etc.

That's the real success that doesn't come from any alcohol, drug, or sensation-seeking addictions. You have elevated yourself with so much hard work.

## 7.6 Overconfidence

When you know that the possibility of happening an event is almost certain because you know it very well or you did the same thing various times, then it might be possible that you may overlook something. Without properly analyzing the associated risk in that matter, you decide to take action. It may be possible that you already succeeded many times but every associated risk requires your full attention. You need to analyze every nook and corner carefully and cannot overlook anything.

Whatever unknown is coming, it always needs your attention. Whatever work demands vigilance, you will have to give it. You should not put your mind in the sleep zone just because you are already well aware of it. Due to overconfidence, many people make big mistakes that they did not expect.

In the stock market, after initial successes, some people start taking large trading positions without properly analyzing the risk involved. Due to overconfidence, sometimes they ignore even the most important things. If you succeed in one strategy it is not necessary that success will be ensured the next time also. While doing the work, even if everything remains constant, it should not be forgotten that time has changed. Whatever hard work you put in the first time, you need to do the same or more again.

If circumstances are changing put your mind in an alert zone, do all necessary research whatever you can do. Do not ignore anything, if you keep your mind in the sleep zone then chances of failure are high.

## 7.7 Feeling Safe

People feel safe doing things when they see others doing the same thing. Like, making the same type of investments, buying the same shares that their friends have bought, buying the same type of products, buying the same type of flats, etc.

What are they doing in these circumstances? They are sending their mind to the sleep zone.

In day-to-day circumstances, our life provides us a great opportunity to put our minds in an alert zone. But due to lethargy many of them easily give up the chance which their life provides in these circumstances.

Whether you like to buy the same product or you want to do the same kind of investment, don't do it blindly. Without proper understanding, you should not proceed to accept it.

### 7.8 Take Risk but in a Limited Manner

The person who takes risks in a limited way, his personality gradually becomes agile and his mind becomes active. You can feel the zest while meeting with them. They look more confident than others. There is no meaning of boredom, frustration, and depression in their life.

On the other hand, doing anything more than necessary causes damage. If you are frequently looking for sensation then you become an adrenaline addict, such behaviour can lead to more harm than benefit. The unknown circumstance is not always in your favour. One wrong step can put you in serious difficulty which can significantly impact your life.

The unforeseen opportunities may suddenly come in front of you if you accept the risk and decided to go ahead. Because walking on an unknown path with full alertness, your mind may be able to catch a new thing that already you have not recognized. But you should consider the consequences at first before taking any action and your mind must be ready to face the unknown.

Cross-examination of all the available facts and figures can put your mind to take the risks in a limited way. It is good to prioritize the order of taking a risk before doing anything on the unknown path. It gradually trains your mind and prepares you to prevent failures.

Taking risks that require alertness and are not harmful to the body is beneficial to mental health and well-being. It makes you more confident and helps you stand out from the crowd. However, addictions are harmful, because every time you can't be fully aware. One minor mistake can change your life forever.

As you mature, it is good to gradually increase the level of risk by setting new goals which you can easily achieve. Develop new skills that require your attention and hard work. Visiting new places help your mind to reinvigorate with novel experiences. Reading new books, learning new hobbies, even learning new software requires a lot of attention.

Once you've mastered one direction, you should never put yourself in the sleep zone again. Otherwise, the dust of time accumulates on the skill. One should move on to learning another new skill, it's a journey of a lifetime where we face new risks at every step and our mind moves on a journey of alertness.

These unknown paths require your attention which always keeps your mind alert where the pleasure of uncertainty is waiting. Success in life means getting out of all addictions, boredom, frustration, and depression where your mind is always in a state of pleasure and ecstasy.

## Key Points

- A path you haven't already taken is always risky.
- The unknown is always a danger and our mind becomes alert where there is danger.
- When your life offers you the opportunity to keep your mind in the alert zone, accept it.
- Don't ignore anything even you already know. Each associated risk requires your full attention.
- Develop new skills that require your focus and hard work, which will put your mind in the alert zone.

# Part II

# Investment

## Chapter-8

# How to Evaluate a Company –I : Qualitative Analysis

It is essential to select a fundamentally strong company for wealth creation for the long term. By buying stocks you are going to invest your money in a business that you believe will flourish in the days to come. On this topic many authors have already made strong arguments that you must understand the business of a company thoroughly before investing. You should not invest a single penny in any company unless you understand its business model.

### 8.1 Sources of Revenue

Before putting your hard-earned money in any stock, you must know at which source the company is generating revenue. Legendary investor Warren Buffet has said that “Never invest in a business you cannot understand.”

It is good to focus on only those companies about which you can understand the source of revenue better. Because each person has a limit to understand the types of business and it depends on what background he is coming from, what is his education, what is his area of interest, etc. There are many companies listed on the stock exchanges and you cannot understand the business model of each one and if you are not able to understand it then it is good to leave it.

Once you understand the source of revenue then you will be able to gauge it and can understand the fluctuations of it. Otherwise, you will always depend on the advice of others as what to do next. Every day you will see the share price, if the prices are up then there will be greed, if the prices are low then there will be fear. Long-term wealth creation is a long journey and you can’t do it on the shoulders of others.

## 8.2 Subsidiary is not Eating the Parent Company

You have selected a company and decided to do further analysis for investment. This kind of analysis requires your intelligence and time. Before embarking on all these exercises, it is good to take a look at its subsidiaries. If there is no sign of trouble then you can proceed to further analysis. If the company has a subsidiary that is eating away of the parent company's profitability and you haven't already analyzed it, all your effort will be in vain.

## 8.3 Analyze Sales

To evaluate sales, analyze the following key points;

- Historical number of sales and its growth, identify from where it is coming from.
- What products and services are they offering?
- Company's current market share and trends.
- In which geographic region the company is operating.
- Who are its major customers and how many years have they been associated with the company?

- How many new customers are added every year?
- From which geographic region are the existing customers and from which region the new customers are coming?

Geographical information will help you identify which culture is supporting the current demand and what kind of new culture are ready to accept the company's products and services.

For example, if a South Indian company is getting new customers from North India, it means that North Indian culture is accepting the company's products and services. Such information is important and requires careful observation of all developments. The expansion may fail if the company fails to analyze the cultural differences between North and South India.

The major objective of a business is to increase revenue and profitability. If the revenue is stagnant or not increasing then it will put a question mark on the existence of the company except large-cap and mature stocks. Therefore, there must be a growth in the sales figures. If the growth is less than double-digit for the long-term (three years or more) then such kind of stock is not good for investment.

## 8.4 Products and Services

Each company provides certain products and services to its customers. The quality of the products and services offered by the company to its customers are important things that need to be analyzed. As an investor, collect the information available from the company's website, its annual report, etc. Check out the responses of customers who have used its products and services. If possible, visit the company's showroom, notice customer reactions to the products and also get feedback from some other people about its products.

But how to check the reaction of big objects like motorcycles, cars, and trucks, etc. Am I going to buy all these items from the market or should I wait for some good reports about these items? The first option is not possible and if you go for the second it will be too late?

So, what is the way to analyze these types of products?

Keep your eyes open while traveling in a city and see how many new models you've seen on the road in a week or a month. This type of attentiveness provides information about the acceptance of the product among the people. The increasing presence of the vehicle on the road gives a clear indication about the acceptance of the new product/model among the people.

For example, the TVS Jupiter scooter had achieved 2.5 million sales in the 5 years since its first launch in the year 2013. Jupiter became the fastest scooter to reach the 1 million sales mark in just 30 months. The visibility of the Jupiter scooter had increased on the Indian roads. The stock price which was hovering around rupees 50 levels in November 2013 had crossed the level of rupees 700 in December 2017.

## 8.5 Competitive Advantage

It is very difficult for any business to stay away from the competition for a long time. When growth opportunities are visible to others, they plan to enter that area. Therefore, the company must have a competitive advantage over others to build leadership for the long term. It could be its patent, its strong research capability, its brand, etc. Anything that is difficult for its competitors to enter.

Warren Buffett believes the "most important" factor to pick a successful investment is judging the durability of a company's competitive advantage or so-called "moat". Warren Buffett says successful investments are often companies that are low-cost producers or that own powerful brands. "The most important thing [is] trying to find a business with a wide and long-lasting moat around it ... protecting a terrific economic castle with an honest lord in charge of the castle," Buffet said.

### 8.6 Company Culture

The culture of the company must be supportive of its employees. A great company always treat their employees as an asset. Employees should be happy to do their job and there should be a strong learning environment at every level of the company. The relationship between employees and management is very important for any growing company as it leads to customer satisfaction.

As an Investor, find out the company's policies for its employees. Loyal and enthusiastic employees are the key pillars of the company's growth.

I am not in favour of the hiring and firing policies of the company.

To create strong pillars, it is necessary that the brick which was put on the first day of the creation of the pillars still must be there for years. If the mason who makes the pillar keeps changing bricks, then who will believe in the strength of such a pillar? Suppose you got information that 50% of the bricks have been changed in a year after commencement of the work, and next year again 50% of the bricks have been changed, then who will believe the strength of that building. In the same manner, many companies want to become a big company but they always keep on changing their valuable employees.

Sometime in my career, when I got a chance to visit the offices of some such companies, I noticed that every time a new employee is sitting. When I asked what happened to the previous person, the management's reply was 'I fired'. But what is the reason for changing employees so often, I asked. Their reasoning is simple, that they are looking for the best talent. That was a general discussion but it has provided a very important clue to me.

These types of employers don't understand what they are doing wrong. Years later, they are still where they started, and they don't understand what went wrong even after putting in so much money, time, and effort.

The concept of positive and negative mental energy also works here. People try to avoid going to hospitals, cremation sites, etc. as they are places of negative energy. In the same way where people are afraid and cry, negative energy is created and this negative energy hinders you to do anything constructive. This is the reason that before starting anything positive it is necessary to clean it with water first.

Similarly, if people always have the fear of losing their jobs, then this creates negative energy in their minds. If more and more people get scared then a lot of negative energy will be created. If you haven't experienced such negative energy then try to experience it, when you enter a room for the first time and you don't feel any kind of positive vibes there. If you are a sensitive person then you are able to catch the change in energy level.

Such fearful people are always interested in saying only one thing – 'Yes Sir'. Because they are always afraid of losing their jobs, therefore, their minds are always wavering. Such kind of employee can't do anything constructive. To create something concrete and constructive you need a very peaceful and stable mind.

For example, suppose a mason is sitting in such a place that is always wavering or the mason's mind is always shaky, then how can he make a strong pillar. In such a situation, they want to finish their work somehow and go back home at the end of the day. Many people do their work this way.

The entire culture of the company should be in such a way that it generates only positive energy. Such energy will automatically uplift the entire organization.

Strong building requires strong pillars, and the strength of strong pillars is that the brick that was attached on the first day of construction of the pillars should last for the life of the building.

## 8.7 Training for Employees

The company should focus on increasing the efficiency of the employees, so training and development are important for any organization as efficiency cannot be built in a day. The company should create a channel for the development of skills of their employees and it should keep it going. As an investor, it is good to focus on those companies which give significance to the training and development of their employees. Many companies focus on training their employees, but for many of them, the expenditure on training is worthless.

A knife always needs to be rubbed, without being rubbed it will become dull after some time. Similarly, training programs hone the skills of the employees. Without which, their sharpness would fade away after some time. Without proper training, if the organization is hoping to increase productivity, it is like sending soldiers to the battlefield without training and rifles.

**Key Points**

- Invest only in companies whose business model you can understand.
- Check the quality of products and services and the responses of customers who use it.
- The entire company culture should be such that it generates only positive energy.
- Training and skill development is another important factor, as knives always need to be sharpened, training programs hone the skills of the employees.

*Chapter – 9*

# How to Evaluate a Company – II: Quantitative Analysis

The financial numbers reflect the performance of a company. As an investor, you need to analyze these financial numbers deeply and carefully. These numbers hold significant meaning and play an important role in the valuation of a stock.

## 9.1 EBITDA

Your selected stock must show positive performance at the EBITDA level. Check the deductions after revenue to arrive at the level of EBITDA. Whether EBITDA is increasing, decreasing, or constant on quarterly or yearly performance, you need to find out which item is playing a major role to arrive at this performance.

If you don't know the reason you cannot catch a change in performance, and you would be surprised if there is any deviation comes from your expectations at EBITDA level. Although there are many other reasons for surprises in the stock market, this can be one and you should not ignore it.

For example, suppose a rise in crude oil prices is putting pressure on paint companies. Because about 50 percent of the raw materials used by paint companies are derivatives of crude oil, which accounts for about 30-35 percent of the total raw material cost of the paint industry. Volatility in crude oil prices may put pressure on the profits of paint companies. Therefore, before investing your money in paint companies you must be aware of the trend in crude oil prices. Read the company notes carefully, how the management is handling the volatility in crude oil prices. When you have this kind of information you are confident about your investment and do not worry about day-to-day fluctuations in stock prices.

## 9.2 Expenditure

Check each item under the expense section and observe its growth at least for the past five years. You will find that these financial numbers are intertwined and there is a connection among them.

For example, if a company's sales are increasing by 10%, its raw material costs, employee expenses, and items that contribute to the increase in sales will also increase by roughly the same proportion. A company cannot achieve higher sales without increasing its raw material consumption. If sales are increasing and raw material costs are also increasing, then this is acceptable. But the fall in sales along with the increase in raw material cost provides a negative signal.

In the same way, a company cannot achieve higher sales without increasing the number of headcounts. There should be rationality between sales and employee spending. It provides information about the increase in salary in the organization if the number of employees is constant and expenditure of the employees has increased. If this growth is in line with sales figures, that's fine. But if sales are declining, the number of employees is falling and employee expenses are rising, examine the salaries of key personnel in the company.

It might be possible that they are misusing their power and taking interest only in their pockets. These types of companies are unable to face the competition in the market and they get wiped out soon.

### 9.3 Net Income

The goal of a company is to generate profit for its shareholders and maximize it over the long run. This figure comes after deducting total expenses, depreciation, and taxes from total revenue. Therefore, an increase in net income is very important to stay invested in a company for a long period.

Take a look at past performance before investing your money, is there a continuation of growth, volatility in performance or are the figures negative? In the case of negative numbers, analyze it carefully from revenue to profit to see which item is dragging performance. If a company shows negative growth in its profits continuously (over the last three years), then it is not a good company to invest in.

Long-term investment requires; patience and careful observation of financial performance every year.

### 9.4 Inventory

Each day of sales is directly related to inventory and affects the company's cash flow. When sales increase, there is a need for a sufficient level of inventory for timely delivery, hence demand estimation is extremely important for the success of any business.

If sales are not growing, high levels of inventory negatively affect cash flow and create an alarming signal. Therefore, a company should clear the existing inventory as soon as possible and should not get stuck with old inventory in warehouses.

If production exceeds sales, the inventory level will rise which will put pressure on cash flow and the company management will have to think of new strategies to increase its sales and clear the existing inventory. The decision to cease production provides a negative signal to the market and will instill fear among existing employees about potential job losses.

On the other hand, if sales exceed production, inventory levels will drop, cash flow will increase, company management becomes optimistic about growth. In these circumstances there is a feeling of enthusiasm and optimism among the employees.

Therefore, while analyzing financial numbers inventory figures are very important. Check the inventory to sales ratio of the company, a sudden increase or decrease in any year demands careful observation of inventory on that year. For smooth functioning, a company must maintain a balance between production, inventory, and sales.

## 9.5 Reserves and Surplus

Take a look at reserves and surplus of the company on the balance sheet. If the reserves are strong and it is increasing every year then it provides a signal of strong health of the company.

After declaring the dividend, the balance amount is transferred to reserves and added under retained earnings. Without the availability of adequate funds, a company cannot go for expansion and cannot achieve the desired growth. Therefore, a young and aggressive company is always interested in increasing reserves and it may be possible that they may not take interest in declaring a dividend. A growing company is always interested in increasing its reserves and this is a strong indication of a growth stock.

Retained earnings come from the net profit minus the total amount of dividends, which belong to the shareholders. Therefore, an increase in reserves is beneficial for the shareholders.

Compare the company's reserves to the size of its equity capital. This type of company is a strong candidate for a bonus if equity capital is low and reserves are increasing every year.

A company should declare its bonus when its business is growing and there is a genuine demand for its shares among the shareholders. Post bonus, the company's equity base increases, proportionally stock price decreases and it encourages retail participation.

When a company announces bonuses unnecessarily or just for financial gimmicks, the demand-supply mismatch of shares leads to a fall in prices, and if the company is not able to expand the business, the demand for shares will not increase, and prices will not go up due to excess supply of shares. Such a move would become a nightmare for the shareholders who bought the stock only because of the bonus announcement.

### 9.6 Risks and Concerns

Every business carries some risk and you need to know the associated risks that can affect the profitability of the company. Without a proper understanding of risk, you cannot make a wise investment decision.

Read the company's annual report and study all the risks involved and its impact on financial performance. If any such situation already happens, try to understand how the company management has dealt with that situation. To collect such information, you need to study up on that year's conference calls.

For example, in tyre stocks fluctuations of raw material prices; Crude oil prices fluctuations are important in paint companies; Steel prices are important for automobile companies; Lead prices are important to battery manufacturers; Information related to monsoon is important for FMCG companies, etc.

**Key Points**

- The company should show positive performance at the EBITDA level.
- Inventory and sales are co-related with each other. Examine these items very carefully and try to identify the connection between them.
- Check the status of reserves every year and a good growth represents a strong health of the balance sheet.
- Be aware of the associated risks that could affect the profitability of the company.

*Chapter – 10*

# How to Evaluate a Company – III : Ratio Analysis

Ratio analysis helps a lot in making sound decisions while investing. In the book of finance, various ratios are written and divided into major categories. Each ratio has its meaning and provides important information. But in this article, I will discuss only a few of them which provide the main clues;

## 10.1 EPS

This is a very well-known investment ratio and calculated as:

Earnings Per Share (EPS) = Profit After Tax / Total No. of Equity Shares Issued

As an investor, if you want to know the earnings of a company on a per-share basis then this ratio will provide such information. When you are looking at the EPS, also look at the diluted EPS as equities may expand in the future. An increasing trend in EPS shows that the company is performing better and it is a true indicator of the returns on your investments.

(Note: Diluted EPS – All convertible securities are changed into equity)

## 10.2 EBITDA and PAT Margins

EBITDA margin measures the company's overall operating profitability.

It is calculated as; EBITDA / Net Sales

If EBITDA margins are higher compared to its peers and increases every year, this represents a more profitable operation of the company.

PAT margin is also known as net margins and calculated as; Net Profit / Net sales

This ratio is used to determine the final profitability of a company on every rupee of sales generated.

If sales are increasing but margins are not increasing it means that the company is facing a problem of increase in expenditure and they need to curb its expenses.

If EBITDA margins are increasing but PAT margins are not increasing it means that the company is facing a problem and need to check every item from EBITDA to PAT that which one is putting pressure on PAT margin.

(This topic is further discussed in Chapter 11: Investment in Growth Stocks)

**10.3 Dividend and Yield**

Discussed in Chapter 12: Understanding the Dividend

**10.4 Debt / Equity Ratio**

Calculated as: Total debt / Net Worth

If the company is aggressive in financing its growth through debt, then the debt-equity ratio is high and results in volatile earnings due to higher interest expenses. It differs in every industry, such as for capital intensive industry like automobiles it is high and for service industry like computer software development, it is low.

This ratio provides vital information about the strength of the balance sheet. How strong is the company's financial position to withstand any headwinds in case of any downturn cycle? In case of business decline, companies with high debt find it difficult to pay their interest and those that manage to make payments are likely to lose creditworthiness.

To finance its projects, the company needs debt that will propel its growth and increase earnings, but a high debt-to-equity ratio translates into higher risk for equity holders.

### 10.5 Book Value Per Share

Book value is the value of the company's assets available on the company's balance sheet and book value per share is calculated as;

> Book Value divided by the total number of outstanding shares of the company.

Suppose a company was to be liquidated, and all of the company's debts have to be paid off, the book value per share represents the amount that shareholders would receive after the liquidation.

The figure of book value represents the actual price when the assets of the company are purchased. The figure on the balance sheet does not reflect the current market value of the company assets. The market price of a stock is usually much higher than its book value, and in any case, if the prices fall below its book value per share, so it shows that either the stock is undervalued and the market is not recognizing its true value or something has gone fundamentally wrong in the company.

### 10.6 Price / Book Value (P/B) Ratio

P/B ratio is calculated as;

> Current market price divided by the book value per share.

If the P/B ratio is more than one it represents that the stock price is more than its assets but if it is less than one then it represents either asset value is higher than the stock price or the company is performing badly and is unable to make proper use of assets.

Book value does not count intangible assets like patents, brand name, etc. therefore this ratio does not provide significant meaning when valuing a service-based firm.

## 10.7 Return on Assets

This ratio provides information about how efficiently the company is utilizing its resources and is calculated as; Net Income divided by Total Assets.

Assets are meant to generate revenue and profitability; therefore, it is the responsibility of a company to generate returns for its assets. But when the question arises to examine the efficiency of management, this ratio provides a clear picture of how efficiently they are using their overall resources to generate returns. The excellence of management can be judged when returns are high but resources are less.

## 10.8 RoE and RoCE

When a company has borrowed money from equity and debt, its responsibility is to generate returns from this capital. These two ratios reveal important information on how efficiently they are utilizing this money. Return on Equity (RoE) calculated as;

Net Income / Shareholder's Fund or Net Worth or Book Value

Return on Capital Employed (RoCE) calculated as;

(EBITDA – Depreciation) / Capital Employed

RoE measures how much return a company makes from shareholders' money, while RoCE tells how much return a company makes on capital employed (Total assets - Current liabilities).

RoE is better when looking for shareholder's investment return and RoCE is better when you are looking for overall profitability of company operations.

These ratios show the profit generated on equity capital and total capital employed. Both ratios play an important role while selecting a stock. When looking for growth stocks both RoE and RoCE should be greater than 15% and should increase every year. If this ratio slips to a single-digit number, the stock will not perform for the long term. When the company has raised money from equity and debt, it is its responsibility to make profits. Therefore, a higher ratio would be more favourable as it means that more profit is generated from each rupee of equity capital and capital employed.

## 10.9 Price / Earnings Ratio (P/E)

Calculated as: Current Market Price (CMP) / Earning Per Share (EPS)

It is a valuation ratio and compares the company's current market price to its per-share earnings. The multiple in P/E refers to how much investors are willing to pay per rupee of earning for the company. If you compare the P/E of one company with that of another, you will get an idea of whether the stock valuation is cheaper or higher. But this comparison should be made in the same industry.

A stock with a high P/E ratio is considered to be a growth stock as investors are expecting higher-earning growth in the future. While a stock with a low P/E signifies, investors have modest expectations about its growth.

(This ratio is further discussed in Chapter - 13: Important rules for buying and selling)

### 10.10 PEG Ratio

The PEG ratio compares a company's P/E ratio to its expected earnings growth rate for a specified time period. One can use the Forward PEG or Trailing PEG method to calculate the ratio.

The yield is usually expressed as a percentage. The theory of PEG says that if the percentage rises above 100% then the stock becomes overvalued, if it is less than 100% then the stock becomes undervalued, and equally represents a fair valuation of the stock.

For example, let the P/E of Stock A be 20 and expected growth is also 20%, then the PEG ratio stands at 100% which is the fair valuation of the stock. Suppose for stock B, P/E is 10 and expected growth is 20%, then PEG ratio comes at 50% (10/20), so the stock is undervalued. For stock C, P/E is 25 and growth is 20% then PEG stands at 125%, the stock is overvalued.

Another thumb rule about the PEG ratio is, if it crosses 200% then it triggers a sell signal and if falls below 50% then it triggers a buy signal. To analyze the past trend, one can use the historical P/E and historical growth rate.

## 10.11 EV / EBITDA

The EV/EBITDA ratio is calculated by dividing the enterprise value (EV) by earnings before interest, taxes, depreciation, and amortization (EBITDA). P/E ratio gives the equity multiple, whereas EV/EBITDA gives the firm multiple. This ratio is also known as 'Enterprise Multiple'.

To check the valuation, compare this ratio with the companies of the same industry. If the valuation comes cheaper of a company in comparison with its industry averages, then we consider it an undervalued stock. But you should not be in a hurry to buy on the thought that such an attractive stock is currently available at a cheaper valuation. Each ratio has its meaning but the decision of buying or selling should not be based on only one ratio.

## 10.12 Market Capitalization to Sales Ratio

This ratio is also known as the price to sales ratio and is calculated as; divide market capitalization of a company by total sales over the past 12 months.

Stock prices can move rapidly in the stock market but it takes time to increase sales. Therefore, it is a useful ratio to measure the valuations whether the stocks have overvalued or not.

P/E ratio measures how much investors are willing to pay per rupee of earnings while market cap (MCap) to sales ratio says how much they are paying per rupee for its sales. A low ratio compared to its peers signifies that the stock is undervalued while a higher than industry average indicates that the stock is overvalued. A very high ratio indicates a warning sign. If a company is making losses, there is no P/E and no dividend yield. Then, this ratio is useful for valuing the firm.

If a company whose sales are constant but profitability is increasing due to other income or a company that has negligible sales but showing profits due to other income, this ratio provides a clear insight about the valuations of such kinds of stocks.

Various other tools are used to check the financial performance of the company, but they are beyond the purview of this book.

***Key Points***

Following are the important parameters to check the financial health of a company:

**EPS:** There must growth in EPS every year

**Margins:** Margins should be in double-digit, more than industry averages, and no pressure on it

**RoE and RoCE:** It should be in double-digit, the higher the better

**RoA:** The company must efficiently utilize its assets. The excellence of management can be judged when returns are high but resources are less.

**Debt:** The interest on debt should not eat the profitability of the company

**MCap to Sales:** It should not abruptly jump than its peers

## *Chapter – 11*

# Investment in Growth Stocks

Growth stock means the company can generate more topline and bottomline growth than its peers over the long term. A strong performance in a year or two doesn't mean it's a growth stock. The stock should have the potential to perform well over a long period of time. These stocks have the potential to increase your investment but they are also risky and it is also very difficult to identify such stocks in the initial stages.

Growth companies have some competitive advantage over their peers and have a unique selling proposition (USP) that attracts a large number of customers. They want to grow faster than their peers so they either pay little or no dividends. They are interested in the expansion so they like to invest their profits back in their business.

Growth stocks tend to be in young and growing companies that have already passed a few steps and are now ready to run. Unlike large-cap stocks, these companies have great potential to expand their business. The strong performance in the topline reflects their expansion, however, each expansion carries its own risk. The company belonging to this category tends to perform better for many years after the initial spurt.

When an investor starts examining stocks, they need to select it based on various financial parameters. But, in growth stocks, you will find that these valuation parameters do not fit your predefined criteria. Sometimes, it may be possible that the valuations of these stocks may be high compared to their peers. Therefore, you should not overemphasize these matrices. If you pay more attention to these multiples. then it may be possible that you may leave the stock. This does not mean that you should not do all these analyses. But it means that other than financial analysis, you have to put more effort to identify a growth stock

Sometimes, growth stocks may be seen as expensive and overvalued. Therefore, many investors hesitate to enter it as it can be a risky investment. Remember, in the long run, the price will increase only when the company's market share increases. When you decide to buy an overvalued stock, it is a good idea to see whether its market share is rising or not. Your investment decision can be wrong if your decision in this direction is not right.

When you are holding a growth stock in your portfolio do not focus more on the small deviation that occurred at the time of the quarterly earnings announcement. Rapid price movement occurs in either direction immediately after the announcement of the results. Many investors may take fresh positions or cut their positions as per their analysis of results.

In such case, price fluctuations are likely to be possible. Rather than focusing on these fluctuations, a seasoned investor tries to find out whether the company's market share has increased or not. What happened to its margins, is there any pressure on raw material prices, what are the changes in the shareholding pattern, what other changes have come on this quarter compared to the previous quarter. Prices do not always rise and will fluctuate. Exit stocks only when there is a clear indication of risk.

## Growth Stocks: How to Identify

### 11.1 Collect Information about Key Management

The decision of the person in the driver's seat is more important than that of any other person in the same vehicle. As an investor, you must collect all publicly available information about the company's management. Examine the background of the CEO and his experience in that business. Suppose, a retail broking company appoints a CEO from an investment banking company, that information immediately raises a red flag in investors' minds because dealing with customers in the retail industry and dealing with clients in investment banking are completely different. Check the background. qualifications, and experience of other key personnel before investment.

No matter how many years it's been since the listing, it is good to study the company's RHP (Red Herring Prospectus). When reading the annual report, examine what management had said in earlier years and where they stand now. Because you are supposed to believe that they are capable enough to fly high.

In case of fluctuations in financial numbers, check the available information about key personnel of the company. Is the same team still running or is there a new change? In case of changes, cross-check the company policies.

### 11.2 Understand the Business Model

Your job as an investor is to understand the entire business model of the company. At what source they are generating revenue and making a profit. Understand its products and services and their business plan to sell the products. Their target customer and customers' acceptance of their products. Consumer confidence about the product should be high, they should be loyal to the products and the number of consumers should increase every year.

Sometimes, new product launches may become a major hit. Every company tries to create a rosy picture about its products and services after the new launches.

But you should not be in a hurry to jump after listening to the media propaganda about the product. Wait for the consumer response after the launch of the product.

The changing behaviour of consumer plays a major role in the success and failure of the product. Therefore, you have to get a real feel of all this, and you cannot understand this by doing research only on computers. You have to walk on the street and visit the showroom to get the details, and if possible, discuss it with the dealers.

### 11.3 Increase in Topline and Bottomline

The success of growth stocks depends on their topline and bottomline performance. There may be a possibility that numbers may fluctuate in the long run, but we need to look at the picture from a holistic perspective and consumer acceptance of its products and services.

Rapid growth is not always good as there is a possibility that the company may stumble with its financial and operational controls. There is no formula to say at what rate the increase is justified. But I have seen that double-digit growth is justified to double the topline numbers in the next five years. For example; TVS Motor fared better after 2013 and more than doubled its sales in the next five years.

### 11.4 Increase in Margins

Margin provides a clear picture of the selection of growth stocks. If margins are increasing and with a strong management team the market share of the company is also increasing. Then this is a great stock to add to a portfolio.

If sales growth is good but operating margins are under pressure, examine expenses and most importantly raw material prices. If raw material prices are rising but there is no pressure on margins, it indicates that management is efficient enough to control costs.

If margins are declining, carefully examine each item under the expense section and try to figure out which one is eating up the margin. Take a closer look at the changing trend of raw material prices. Sometimes, the commodity cycle goes on for a long time and it tests your patience.

(Discussed in Chapter -10: How to Evaluate a Company – III)

### 11.5 The Health of the Balance Sheet

It is very common for companies to take debt for their business operations and especially for expansion. Although, debt/equity ratio varies from industry to industry, if it is 1 to 1.5 then we may consider it normal. If it is more then check its proper utilization and ask questions while attending any investors meet or AGM (Annual General Meeting). High debt than the industry averages indicate an alarming signal. Soon, if the performance does not reflect in its sales, then this debt will become bone of throat for the company. Therefore, timely utilization of debt is very important for a company and it must reflect in its topline growth.

### 11.6 Research and Development

Research and development (R&D) play a vital role in the development of the company. R&D is important not only for engineering and high-tech companies, but it is important for all kinds of products and services. After initial success, long-term sustainability is difficult if the company is not focusing on R&D. High R&D expense doesn't necessarily mean it's a growth stock, to evaluate it's good to observe the historical trend of R&D expenditure with new product launches and revenue growth.

### 11.7 Do not Consider IPOs

A growth company must have a successful track record over the past few years. There are too many risks involved in the IPOs. Sometimes, IPOs perform better but for sustainability very few can run for the long term. After initial performance, many IPOs shattered. All the dreams and excitement about stocks suddenly disappear.

### 11.8 Shareholding Pattern

Now you have done enough research and selected the stock with the belief that it will outperform in the long run. But have you analyzed the people who still have the stock? The analysis of the shareholding pattern is also very important along with other analyses. First, check the promoter's stake in the company for the last two years. A high promoter's stake is considered positive while a low stake means that the promoter himself does not trust his company. Too much promoter's stake is also not a good sign.

An increase in promoter's stake is positive as it reflects an increase in confidence, but always it is not positive. You need to know why the stake has increased. Promoter's stake may increase due to share buyback or any merger activity. Stake decline should also be studied in detail, such as the issue of fresh shares for ESOPs or offloading of shares to a strategic partner.

Now Check the FIIs stake in the company. High FIIs holdings are considered positive as they invest only when they have confidence in the company's prospects. However, a very high stake is not good because you do not know when and for whatever reason they will sell. Even all the fundamentals are positive if FIIs start selling for whatever reason, immediately the stock will take a nosedive and as an investor, you will feel panic and do not know exactly what is happening.

(Further discussed in Chapter 13: Important Rules for Buying and Selling)

## 11.9 Finally, Be Patient

After long research, you have selected the stock and believe that your investment will give you manifold returns in the years to come. For that, you should have enough patience and not monitor the prices on a daily pattern. However, no company can show tremendous performance every year in the long run. The deviation will come at your pre-determined parameters. In such scenarios, observe the behaviour of its loyal customers. Whether the consumer belief about the company is still there or it starts declining.

Growth stocks must have the abovementioned strong drivers to perform consistently over a longer period. These stocks will check your patience but in the long run, they will reward you high.

## Key Points

- Collect all publicly available information about the company's management prior to investment.
- Check consumer feedback after the launch of the new product, you should not be in a rush to buy the stock.
- Check topline and bottomline performance and double-digit growth is justified to double the topline numbers in the next five years.
- Better margins are a good indicator of financial performance.
- Check the company's shareholding pattern.

## *Chapter -12*

# Understanding the Dividend

A dividend is a portion of a company's profits distributed to shareholders as a part-owner of the company. After earning profits management may choose an option to retain it or may distribute a portion of profits as dividends to its shareholders.

However, dividends are not guaranteed and are at the discretion of the Board of Directors. A young company needs to reinvest all of its capital to fuel its growth and may decide not to declare any dividends. But when growth is slow and further expansion is limited, the declaration of a dividend becomes necessary to retain shareholders.

Dividends play an important role while selecting stocks for investment. Investors looking for regular income prefer stocks that have a regular record of dividend payments. But if the company distributes the bulk of its profits as dividends, it lacks sufficient reserves for its future growth.

## 12.1 Declaration of Residual Profits

Declaration of residual profit in the form of a dividend to its shareholders is a clear indication of the financial health of the company. It also signals that the company's growth is slowing and it is time to reward its shareholders. The management sitting in the driver's seat knows the financial prospects of the company better. Therefore, a steady or increasing dividend over the previous year indicates a lot of financial health about the company.

A company's dividend declaration to its shareholders is a tool that investors can use as an indication of the company's prospects. In addition to financial ratios, a clear examination of historical dividends reveals a lot of information about the company's prospects.

## 12.2 Steady and Gradual Increase in Dividend Payment

When a company's potential to grow further becomes limited, management is ready to continue to reward its shareholders and pay handsome dividends. If everything goes smoothly this trend is likely to continue for years. It is good to have such stocks in the portfolio as they not only provide risk-free income but also add value.

When management announces dividends, they know better those investors are watching their policies closely. Volatility in dividend payouts unnecessarily provides any positive or negative signals in the market. Therefore, a steady and gradual increase in dividend payout is a healthy sign and most of the companies adopt this policy.

### 12.3 A Sudden Cut in Dividend

In case of any negative indications about the prospects of the company, the first possible action of management is to save all cash outflows of the company. Therefore, a sudden cut in dividends is a clear indication that the company may face a cash crunch or other challenges soon. A company may skip paying dividends if it plans to reinvest or cover costs.

Hence, an investor should keep a close watch on all developments and it is good to avoid such stocks for the time being. This type of action indicates that an investor needs to examine the financial position of the company further and they cannot take such type of information lightly.

When an established company that is paying dividends at regular intervals suddenly increases it, decreases it, or defaults in paying dividends, an investor should examine all the scenarios.

For example, suppose a company is declaring dividends every year and this trend is increasing. The financial health of the company is good and the stock is also performing well. Let us assume that the dividend trend of this company for the last few years is 40%, 60%, 75%, 90%, 100%, 120%, 140%; But the next year suddenly the company takes a deep cut and it declared a dividend of 40%. This indicates that the company is trying to save existing funds for any uncertainties that may arise shortly.

It's also not a very healthy sign if a company suddenly increases its dividend. Because then it will be difficult for them to maintain the same performance. In the example above, let's say that instead of a deep cut next year, the company announced a huge jump in a dividend payment of 1000%. Such kind of hefty payment cannot continue in the years to come. In such cases, the situation of dividend payment is not smooth and declaration of dividend is not normal. This unusual action demands further scrutiny of such kind of announcement.

Because dividends provide a signal of a company's financial health, most companies are hesitant to reduce the amount already declared in the previous year. Even after facing problems from many fronts, the company does not want to give any negative signals in the market, hence, they continue with their stable dividend policy.

However, every reduction in dividend does not give a negative signal about the company, neither increase provides a positive signal. There are times when a company continues to pay a stable dividend and is not able to increase even for years.

**The Bottom Line**

Dividends provide a lot of valuable information about the company. The study of historical dividends provides a clear indication of a company's financial health. When a company suddenly cuts a dividend, it's time to examine all developments as it may indicate that a problem may be brewing in the near future.

A company cannot keep growing forever, ups and downs are part of the business. Dividends provide a lot of valuable information about the company. This cannot be easily overlooked when analyzing a stock.

**Key Points**

- Analyze the trend of dividend, whether it is increasing, stagnant or declining.
- Sudden cut in dividend payment creates concern about the performance of the company. At the same time, a huge jump in dividend payments calls for further scrutiny.

## *Chapter-13*

# Important Rules for Buying and Selling

Knowing the rules of when to buy and when to sell helps us make decisions at the important moment. Here, I will share some of my experiences working with different organizations:

### 13.1 Volume Plays an Important Role

Volume plays an important role in the price movement of stocks. Without an increase in volume, it is difficult for stock price to rise. Therefore, when the volume is increasing, it is a clear indication that momentum is coming here. Low volumes indicate that market participants are not interested in such stocks.

When looking at the chart, this type of activity refers to a gradual accumulation of stocks when there is an increased trading volume and there is very little stock price movement. Such movement does not happen every day. Sometimes it will test your patience and the movement of stocks may take time. But increased volume at the bottom never gives a wrong signal. When fundamentals are also strong in such a stock, do not exit after taking some percentage profit. I have observed that such stocks have performed very well in the long run as long as the fundamentals remain intact.

Similarly, when the trading volume is rising at the top and the prices are also hitting new highs every day, exit such stocks too soon, the downside is imminent. I noticed that high volume at the top with a big price movement in a single day is a clear exit signal. Buying such stocks at the top can be a big mistake if the delivery percentage is also decreasing and the prices are getting higher every day. Here, don't be confused by the price movement caused by strong demand.

### 13.2 Holding of Promoters/FIIs

One thing is certain that if promoters are increasing their stake, they are bullish on their stock and also signifies that they have confidence in their company. Don't buy any shares blindly just because the stake of the promoters or FIIs have gone up. Gather as much information as possible about changes in shareholding patterns. It may be possible that fundamentals start changing on such types of stocks. But you should not rush to buy stocks immediately after having such information. On the other hand, immediately exit the shares where the promoters are selling their stake in the open market. I have seen that those stocks are highly vulnerable in the market if the promoter's holding is less than 30%.

(Discussed in Chapter – 11: Investment in Growth Stocks)

### 13.3 Cheap and Expensive Stocks

In my career, I used to get feedback from various branch managers after writing a research report that - " The stock you recommended is very expensive and people are not taking any interest by looking at the current market price. No matter the fundamentals are strong and the long-term performance is good, but when the prices are high, people are not interested. Why don't you write research reports on those stocks where the prices are below rupees 100 and the stock has the potential to be a multibagger."

I remained silent.

But this is the psychology of many investors that they look at the prices first and are hesitant to buy any expensive stock. Such people are always interested in low-priced stocks. I have looked at the portfolios of many investors and I have found that over sixty percent of the total portfolio consists only of cheap stocks with poor fundamentals.

People are reluctant to buy those stocks where prices are high and eager to enter those stocks where prices are cheap, and with a very strange logic – 'This stock story everyone knows, I want something other. But they forget one more argument – 'Who says something other means cheap stocks.'

I realized that wearing special clothes alone does not make one feel special. Keeping stock of 'Something Important' those others don't know, or even keeping news of 'Others don't know' also gives some people a sense of speciality. I have noticed a sense of conceit in people who are always on the lookout for something more secret. Such people think that they are so important people that they do not keep stocks for the public whose information is known by all, they hold only special stocks or those stocks whose secret information is not known to anyone else according to their opinion.

## 13.4 Be Careful on Valuation Matrix

Sometimes investors place so much emphasis on valuation metrics that they will consider entering a stock only if the valuation is cheap. These valuation parameters provide an important piece of information as to whether a stock is to be considered, but none of it can be looked at in isolation. It should be seen in its full context. Many times, it happens that the valuations of the stocks are cheaper than their peers, but they are unable to perform as they lack the required fundamental triggers.

There are three important valuation parameters we use to analyze a stock;

i) P/E

ii) P/B

iii) EV/EBITDA

P/E: There is so much discussion on this ratio in the market because many investors are only aware of this ratio. Due to their superficial knowledge, they are interested in stocks where P/E is low. But a low P/E only means a stock is undervalued, it doesn't mean that it is good for investing and a high P/E only means the stock is overvalued, it also doesn't mean that it is not good for investment.

The decision to invest money in stock should not be based solely on one valuation parameter that you have selected the stock simply because the valuation is cheap. Even though all the important parameters are saying valuations are cheap, it's not worth putting your money in, if you can't find any fundamental triggers in the stock.

(For P/B and EV/EBITDA read Chapter -10; How to Evaluate a Company – III)

### 13.5 Take a U-Turn

Even after doing various analyses, it is not necessary that your investment decision will be 100% correct. When you realize that you are on the wrong track, take a U-turn immediately.

For example, while driving when people realize that they are on the wrong path, they immediately get perplexed and look for the next available U-turn. There is no argument that I have come such a long way, spent so much time here, now how can I take a U-turn. No, the moment you realize that you are on the wrong track, change your path immediately.

But in the investment world, people hold on to their wrong investments for years, even after knowing that not just the way, everything has gone wrong here. When you come to know that your decision has gone wrong in a particular stock, you should immediately take a U-turn so that your portfolio is oriented in the right direction i.e., it should give you good returns over time.

**Key Points**

- Check the volume of the stock
- Get rid of the mindset of buying cheap and low-priced stocks.
- Don't put too much emphasis on valuation metrics
- When you realize that you are on the wrong path, take a U-turn immediately

# Conclusion

Investing requires not only strong knowledge of the fundamentals but also a deep understanding of the psychology of the market. We learned in earlier chapters how human psychology affects deeply the matters related to money and how it varies from person to person. It also varies for the same person because as his level of knowledge increases, it is not necessary that he should repeat the same decision which he had taken some time ago under certain circumstances. Therefore, the complexity is always high, and the repetition of the action almost becomes impossible. Every time the situation is new and every time the investor has to take a new decision. This is the reason market is always vibrant and alive.

No one wants to live in uncertainty and money provides certainty for the future. Every time a person takes a decision on the responsibility of his shoulders, it strengthens his personality. It is necessary for a person to take independent decisions but his surroundings, prejudices and attachments affect it. Therefore, it is essential for a person to take the right decision and not let such influences affect his decision. I discussed these topics in detail with some other important points that sometimes why it is necessary to be reluctant to take the first step as second step could be costly for you.

Unforeseen circumstances put a person in trouble and sudden loss of money is a serious difficulty that a person may have to face sometimes in his life. But knowing what to expect and how our mind works helps us to better understand and overcome such situations in life.

Experience is needed to understand market psychology, so one should not rush to make quick profits, or else he may fall into the trap and incur losses. Positive and negative triggers come and go, but it is the sentiment that drives the market up and down. The market always moves with expectations and discounts everything, so an investor needs to understand what the majority of investors and traders are thinking in a certain condition.

It is not easy to decide when to buy and when to sell in the equity market. Sometimes everything looks good in the market. This does not mean that you should not follow the rules of investing. The allure of big money attracts while the fear of losing it gives you a second thought. There is always a dilemma about where to invest and what to sell and there is only one way to get out of the state of confusion - 'Increase your understanding'.

Making money in stocks requires a lot of research and a good understanding of the market. Market volatility is always there but if you follow the rules then you can reduce the chances of risks of your investment.

I hope this book helps you learn more about the human psychology related to investing and how to make a sound decision when a critical situation arises.

# Bibliography

Investment Psychology Explained by Martin J. Pring, John Wiley & Sons, Inc., New York

Contrarian Investment Strategies: The next generation by David Dreman, Simon & Schuster, New York

Trading to Win, The Psychology of Mastering the Markets, Ari Kiev, John Wiley & Sons, Inc.

Quotefancy <https://quotefancy.com/quote/996901>Accessed 04 June 2021

"Dot-com bubble"<https://en.wikipedia.org/wiki/Dot-com_bubble>Accessed 15 June 2021

"But They Did Not Give Up" <https://www.uky.edu/~eushe2/Pajares/OnFailingG.html>Accessed 15 June 2021

"The Psychology of Risk-Taking", Goodthepary <https://www.goodtherapy.org/blog/risks-adrenaline-benefits-neuroticism-0418137> Accessed 06 July 2021

"Are You a Risk Taker", Psychology Today <https://www.psychologytoday.com/intl/articles/200011/are-you-risk-taker> Accessed 06 July 2021

"What Is Dopamine", WebMD<https://www.webmd.com/mental-health/what-is-dopamine>Accessed 07 July 2021

"The Psychology of Risk-Taking And How To Control It", BIT REBELS<https://bitrebels.com/lifestyle/psychology-risk-taking-control/> Accessed 07 July 2021

"Why We Take Risks", Psychology Today, <https://www.psychologytoday.com/us/blog/media-spotlight/201412/why-we-take-risks> Accessed 07 July 2021

"Epinephrine", Britannica, <https://www.britannica.com/science/epinephrine> 08 July 2021

"Adrenaline", Wikipedia, <https://en.wikipedia.org/wiki/Adrenaline>08 July 2021

https://www.bseindia.com/

https://www.investopedia.com/

"From the Desk of Warren Buffett", <https://www.intelligentim.com/from-the-desk-of-warren-buffet>13 July 2021

Financial Express, <https://www.financialexpress.com/auto/bike-news/tvs-jupiter-achieves-2-5-million-sales-in-5-years-what-made-honda-activa-rival-taste-this-milestone/1246099/> Accessed 23 July 2021

"Investing", CNBC, <https://www.cnbc.com/2018/05/07/warren-buffett-believes-this-is-the-most-important-thing-to-find-in-a-business.html> 17 July 2021

"Raw Material Issues In Indian Paint Industry", CoatingsWorld,https://www.coatingsworld.com/issues/2020-01-01/view_india_asia_pacific_reports/raw-material-issues-in-indian-paint-industry/ Accessed 22 July 2021

# About The Author

Ajay Srivastava is the founder of www.lotuswisdom.in and holds 'Bachelor of Science' from Deen Dayal Upadhyay Gorakhpur University, Gorakhpur (UP) and 'Masters Programme in International Business' from PSG Institute of Management, Coimbatore (Tamil Nadu).

He has extensive experience in the capital market as a Lead Analyst, Investment Banker, Consultant, and Advisor in identifying investment opportunities and formulating strategies. In his career, he has written various research notes and has done in-depth research from a commercial and financing point of view in multiple deals. With diverse industry experience and wide understanding, he started imparting his knowledge in the industry since 2013. He works as a Consultant and Corporate Trainer.

He has deep knowledge of graphology and since childhood he is very much interested in analyzing a person by handwriting and has analyzed the handwriting of hundreds of persons in his life.

Nowadays he is very much passionate to learn about astrology in deep and has completed a Two-year Certificate Course - 'Jyotirvid' in Astrology from Bharatiya Vidya Bhavan, Mumbai.

Email ID: ajay.srivastava@lotuswisdom.in

Web Site: http://www.lotuswisdom.in/

# Notes

# Notes